The timeliness of this book, the complexity and sensitivity of its subject matter, and the precision with which Islamic knowledge and understanding are offered in it as reasonable remedies and conclusions for problems facing Man, speak to the importance and need for a common-sense voice of faith and reason in this apparent season of troubles and divisiveness in the global human society. Where sweeping and powerful social trends are straining the moral and intellectual resources of world leaders, and stretching the patience of the common man, clear steps to freedom, peace, security, and a realization of a just order in respective nations are supremely valued by citizens of the world in every country and on every continent.

With *On Nature and Nations: The Muslim-American Message for Humanity in the Day of Religion* Earl Abdulmalik Mohammed's reasoning rings with a familiar language and distinction. This compilation of nine speeches adhere to the unmistakable disciplines of Islam in the tradition of the late Muslim-American leader, W. Deen Mohammed. They offer sensible perspectives and answers for peoples in crisis. Addressing the most pressing issues of the Day -immigration, nationalism, race and ethnic tension, patriotism, and the moral uses of knowledge and wealth, Earl Abdulmalik Mohammed speaks with the humility of a servant of G'd and man, delivering on behalf of Muslim-Americans, a message of healing and salvation to an America and world in need. This book is compelling. It makes the argument that the Muslim-American voice is not only living and viable, but a necessary contribution to Man's discussions on his present condition and his own good future.

On Nature and Nations

The Muslim-American Message for
Humanity in the Day of Religion

"Your Creation and your Resurrection are in no
manner except as a single Soul"

Holy Qur'an 31:28

EARL ABDULMALIK MOHAMMED

PUBLISHED BY BILALIAN RIVERS PRESS, A SUBSIDIARY OF BILALIAN RIVERS MEDIA LLC

"When the responsibility for the trust, in care of the people, is turned over to those unqualified; then expect the Hour."

~Muhammed the Prophet

On Nature and Nations

The Muslim-American Message for Humanity in the Day of Religion

"Your Creation and your Resurrection are in no manner except as a single Soul"

Holy Qur'an 31:28

EARL ABDULMALIK MOHAMMED

On Nature and Nations

The Muslim-American Message for
Humanity in the Day of Religion

Published March, 2019

BILALIAN RIVERS PRESS
A Subsidiary of BILALIAN RIVERS MEDIA LLC
   Bilalian Rivers Media is a duly registered Limited Liability
   Corporation in the State of North Carolina.

www.bilalianriverspress.com

Cover Design and Concept: Azizah H. Mohammed, Earl Abdulmalik Mohammed

Manuscript Preparation: Bilal Yasin El-Amin, Abdul-Hafeez Waheed, Robin Surface

ISBN: 978-1-7336034-0-9 (hardcover)

ISBN: 978-1-7336034-1-6 (soft cover)

Printed in the United States of America.

"We are looking for powerful and big solutions. We are looking for a Mujeddid, saint, genius to be born... We are looking for a person who will solve great complicated problems for us. All we need is a person with good common sense to say: "Let us not be hypocrites by each other. Let us accept One G'd, one creation, one people, and let us work for the good of all people. It is as simple as that."

~ Imam W. Deen Mohammed

Author's Note About the Cover:

What is the Time of the new heavens and the new earth? What is the *Day of Religion?* The cover of this book intends to illustrate an Age in which the human soul is challenged by its own declared aspirations in confrontation with its inherent nature.

The Day of Religion is an important reference from the Holy Qur'an and Muhammed the Prophet's teaching focusing attention on spiritual truths and language identifying and affecting the consciousness, behaviors, and choices of all human Communities. It refers to a conclusion in human society where all peoples are driven, by the onset of clear universal truths and awesome social developments, to the recognition that mankind's artificial world of distinctions and barriers will not escape a reckoning. It is the Day that answers the question as to whether a man should be his brother's keeper. In that Day no nationality, race, creed, or class of human beings will have accrued a special status or immunity from its Determinations.

Leading to that Day the message will come clear that political, economic, cultural, and spiritual perspectives which wantonly seek to exploit human divisions, ultimately weaken humanity, and promise to upend all unjust notions of world order. It is the Day where the human community will be compelled to witness and recognize that its knowledge is woefully finite, and that which illuminates its world is only a gray shade borrowed from the Divine Light and Divine Knowledge which sets the true understanding and balance of Universal Justice.

This Conclusion is a new reality for humanity, and it is a dawning of new possibilities for the human world. In Islamic teaching the Merciful Benefactor and Merciful Redeemer -Lord-Creator of all Systems of Knowledge, is the Owner of the *Day of Religion*. His Sole Authority will expose humanity's uses of myth and science, and judge their accountability for any betrayals of Truth. In the moments announcing this Day, the Merciful Redeemer opens to every human soul a pathway of reconciliation and redemption, but that soul must humble itself to read and obey the Signs. Among those Signs are the moon that reflects Light, but cleaves; mountains which stand firm for a term, but crumble; and trees that feed and write. But, foremost are the Signs in man's own human self: those human habitations and constructions which house man's zones of liberty or oppression, and which define his boundaries of justice and injustice.

"On that Day man will say: Where is the refuge?"

Holy Qur'an: 75:10

For Parents and Children who seek their dignity of human birthright in refuge: may they meet with the relief of G'd's Mercy, the support and care of His Devotees, and the respect of an honorable citizenship in just nations

About the Author

Earl Abdulmalik Mohammed has been a distinguished spokesman for Islam and Muslim affairs for over a quarter century. He is a lifelong student of Islamic knowledge, and an accomplished instructor of religion and scriptural sciences. He has earned advanced credits in international and Arabic language studies from the Middle East Institute, Georgetown University, and the Modern Arabic Language Institute of Yemen in Sana'a. He served for fifteen years as the National Representative for Imam W. Deen Mohammed and his Ministry, the leader of the largest Muslim community in the Western hemisphere. In that capacity he addressed congregations at mosques, churches, and synagogues, made presentations to government representatives and bodies, participated in formal discussions with political, cultural, and social leaders and organizations, and lectured at dozens of colleges and universities throughout North America. On behalf of Imam W. Deen Mohammed and the Muslim-American community he traveled to meet with leaders in Africa, Europe, the Middle East and Asia, and participated in conferences and programs in Saudi Arabia, Malaysia, Ethiopia and Italy, among other countries. He has been interviewed by major print and electronic media, and written several articles on Islam in America, including an *"Open Letter to all Americans,"* that appeared in *USA Today* shortly after the September 11 attacks.

When Imam W. Deen Mohammed announced his resignation as leader in the society of Muslim-Americans, some major U. S. newspapers speculated Earl Abdulmalik Mohammed to be his logical successor:

"Influential Leader Steps Down," (The Los Angeles Times, September 13, 2003); *"A Journey of Faith,"* (The Baltimore Sun, August 16, 1998). In December 2001 at a public forum in Grand Rapids, Michigan Imam Mohammed was asked if there were any persons from his community who could represent Islam and Muslims the way he did. He said in response, *"Earl Abdulmalik Mohammed, in my opinion, is responsible for most of the propagating of the true image of Muslims in America. Not just for us, but for all Muslims"* (The Muslim Journal Newspaper, December 14, 2001).

In 2013 Earl Abdulmalik Mohammed was convicted of a single count of mail fraud related to his family business. He is currently serving a U. S. federal prison sentence.

In 2016 he authored *Democracy, Civic Virtue, and Islam: The Muslim-American Jihad Against Extremism* to wide international distribution and acclaim. With *On Nature and Nations: The Muslim-American Message for Humanity in the Day of Religion* his voice is established as the foremost spokesman for Islam in America in the guided tradition of Imam W. Deen Mohammed.

Earl Abdulmalik Mohammed's speeches, writings, and podcast interviews are available to the public at www.eamspeaks.com.

Acknowledgments

We thank Allah, the Merciful Benefactor, the Merciful Redeemer, the Mighty and Sublime. Highly Glorified is He, Lord-Cherisher-Sustainer-Guardian-Evolver of all the Systems of Knowledge. Guarantor of Faith and all sacred Trusts. Owner of all that exists. Author of Religion, its teaching, and its laws. Pardoner of sins. No vision can grasp Him, and yet He is Ever-Watching over all. No fatigue governs Him and He does not rest or sleep. He is not created but is Creator of everything. Originator of Nature, Revealer of Guidance, Dispatcher of Prophets and Messengers, Bestower of every kindness on His creation. We praise Him, the Preserver and Increaser of all favors, Hearer and Grantor of prayers. We witness that He alone, deserves worship and nothing is partner with Him in the Rule of all He has created. We witness that Muhammed is His Messenger, the perfected and completed human being. To him, the Book of Guidance with no defects -the Holy Qur'an, was revealed and entrusted. Muhammed is the standard of conduct and character for human life, and a mercy to all creation. We pray the choicest blessings of Allah be on him, and the peace. And we pray Allah's favor on Muhammed's family and his companions, and all of the righteous leaders and followers through the ages until today. Amen.

I thank Allah for my parents, family, and close associates. Their love and support are strong, consistent, and lasting. I ask Allah to preserve and protect them.

I am grateful for the hardworking and dedicated members of the Muslim-American Conference for Human Salvation. My heart leans to singling each one of them out for their unique skills, contributions, and assistance. They are each blessed persons and leaders, and together they form an honorable, determined group of Believing men and women. May Allah reward them with the Best of this Life and the Best of the Hereafter.

We are thinking of our late leader, the Guided-Reformer and the Imam of al-Islam. Our religion does not encourage embellishment or sentimentalism. It values Truth above all else. The straight truth is that Islam in the West would not have Islamic knowledge or identity to construct an Islamic life and destiny upon were it not for Imam W. Deen Mohammed. We exist as a dignified and viable People because of what Allah inspired him to give us, may Allah Grant him the Mercy.

Allah, the Most High, Praised is He above all, accepts and supports only the good. We turn to Him and we put our trust in Him for acceptance of our works and all good results.

Preface

Praise be to Allah. We witness that nothing is deserving of worship except Him, the Lord and Creator of all that exists, all systems of knowledge. We seek His Forgiveness, His Protection, His Help and His Favor. We witness that Muhammed is His Messenger. He is the Universal Messenger and a Mercy to all Creation. We ask Allah's Choice Favor on Muhammed and we salute him. We salute his family and companions. We are thankful to Allah for our history and tradition in the religion of al-Islam in America. We thank Him for our good and promising Islamic future. We ask Allah's Mercy on all of those who preceded us and made the contributions that permit us to stand now as Muslims obeying Allah in the teaching of the Holy Qur'an and tradition of Muhammed the Prophet. We ask Allah's Mercy on the foremost of those, the Imam of al-Islam, the Guided-Reformer, Imam W. Deen Mohammed.

This book is the inaugural publication of *Bilalian Rivers Press*. *Bilalian Rivers Press* is dedicated to publishing works that serve humanity through Islamic knowledge and expression, and the excellence of the Muslim-American soul, mind, and experience in religion, education, the natural sciences, business, and culture. We intend to seek and support those of our creative Muslim-American thinkers and aspiring authors by endeavoring to bring their works to press. *Bilalian Rivers Press* intends to publish works in the Islamic spiritual, social, economic, legal, and cultural sciences and genres. This includes scholarly works, educational texts for elementary and high school curriculums, books of poetry, cookbooks, children's and young adult literature, news and information publications, and novels. *Bilalian Rivers Press* will bring to the printed medium that which best serves progress for human community in the way that Islamic teachings intend, with particular devotion to encouraging Muslim-African-American scholarship, artistry, and literary excellence.

With this Preface, Bilalian Rivers Press is very pleased to introduce our first important project: *On Nature and Nations: The Muslim-American Message for Humanity in the Day of Religion.* This book is a compilation of nine speeches that Earl Abdulmalik Mohammed delivered during the year 2018 while he continued to serve a United States federal prison sentence for a one-count mail fraud conviction. The speeches compiled here were intended by him as public addresses on subjects demanding the attention of all citizens of the world. He prepared them in response to persons throughout the United States who trusted his Islamic understanding and sought his opinion and counsel on these various religious and social issues.

Ranging from such important subjects as immigration, nationalism, race-relations, patriotism, inter-faith cooperation, wealth and economies, ethnic tensions, to other compelling international and universal social trends straining the moral and intellectual resources of leaders and common people alike, these nine speeches reflect a responsible and high level grasp of historical truths, and a highly-skilled use of what has been described as the "guided tradition and language" of Imam W. Deen Mohammed. In these moments for human society which many describe as 'troubled and divisive', the timeliness of this compilation, the complexity and sensitivity of its subject matter, and the precision with which Islamic knowledge and understanding are offered as reasonable conclusions, points not only to the author's special intellect, but also reveals something of the faith, courage, and determinations in the man in spite of the constraints he endures as a United States federal prisoner.

In these nine speeches, Earl Abdulmalik Mohammed's logic is distinctly reminiscent of the great African-American social and spiritual identity re-construction work associated with the Honorable Elijah Muhammad. His reasoning strictly obeys Islamic emphasis, and he distinguishes himself as the foremost spokesman and representative for the language and leadership tradition of Imam W. Deen Mohamed's religious and social teaching. We observe that this combination is rare, if it exists at all in one person anywhere else. We assert that it has not been witnessed with this ability or level of fluency since Imam Mohammed. It may well be determined in the years ahead that this book signaled the rise of Earl Abdulmalik Mohammed as the ideological successor of W. Deen Mohammed, and the next consequential leader from among the Muslim-American people.

We, the Publisher -*Bilalian Rivers Press*, by virtue of the principles we are committed to cannot excuse ourselves from recognizing the seriousness of these Times. Thus, we are compelled to present this book and vigorously promote its author. While we understand that the evidence of the value of this book is with G'd's Decision and the witness of responsible citizens in all nations, it is our duty to commend its content as the author did when he first delivered these speeches: To the good service of mankind, with regard, trust, and love for G'd and humanity.

The Publisher
December 10, 2018

Table of Contents

Author's Note About the Cover xi

About the Author xv

Acknowledgments xvii

Preface xix

Introduction xxv

Part I: Nature and Language

1   A New Language of Liberty 1

2   Poisoning the Wheat Harvest 11

3   The Sacred Entitlements 27

Part II: Nations and Just Society

4   War on Innocence 43

5   Crisis in Muslim Leadership 55

6   Salvation for America 63

Part III: On Nature and Nations

7   Nationalism is an Evil 83

8   Muhammed the Prophet is Nearest to
    Jesus the Christ 101

9   A New People 119

Special Note from the Author 135

Statement on March 15, 2019 New Zealand Attacks 141

Index 143

Introduction

This question was posed to Earl Abdulmalik Mohammed in December 2017:

Question: I know that you have not spoken on any public issues in awhile. I thought that given the seriousness of the issue that many people would benefit from your thoughts on the moving of the American Embassy in Israel from Tel-Aviv to Jerusalem.

Answer: I must say that I would be much more at ease addressing this question as a free citizen. I hope you will ask this of me again when I am free. I do plan to speak to these concerns representing our Islamic tradition that would be issues that the late leader of our tradition and community -Imam W. Deen Mohammed would not have ignored once I am free.

It is important and complex especially for its direct implications of those whose lives will be at risk or affected because of it. For us, the Bilalian people or African-American community of Muslims in the following of Muhammed the Prophet and those following the guided tradition of Imam Warithuddin Mohammed, we should be perceiving it from Islamic teachings and also our affinity for the causes and suffering of oppressed peoples and the issues of justice that are due or are the entitlement of all human beings and human communities. The Palestinian people are in my thoughts and prayers and I am also aware of and thinking of the so-called Rohingya -a Muslim people of Burma who have been displaced - and I say so-called Rohingya because I do not know that they approve of this identification, and all who have been made weak by the schemes against their human life and dignity.

The modern city as we understand it now is not the focus of Islamic teachings, that is the present-day city of Jerusalem. But what is in focus is that place that the Muslims call Al-Quds as an orientation for our human life as described in our religions or traditions of faith. That may be surprising for some who are not familiar with Islamic teaching. What I mean is the life we believe G'd planned for all of us to enjoy as human beings in this existence we have on this earth. That precinct that the Muslims have called Haram Shareef and the Qur'an calls Masjid al-Aqsa is a representative space for those who believe that G'd loves, respects, and planned the best life for humanity.

Allah says in the Qur'an that that place is a blessed place and that it is associated with the light of understanding for man's purpose and that it is a sign of that enlightenment. What I am saying now is directly from the Qur'an. It is a blessed place and that blessing is for all people, not one or another people. That blessing is not or cannot be claimed by one people to the exclusion of another. It is to us a symbol for Islam's view of the universal rights and destiny of man on this earth. We all share in these blessings, and we would say that the religious communities that cherish the tradition of guidance we have in revealed knowledge -our Holy Books, are the custodians to guarantee or secure these blessings in society.

This is why other nations in the world do not place their embassies there. They are saying that place is not exclusive to the state of Israel, it belongs to all people. Those nations are saying our relationship with the state of Israel is a separate matter from our recognition of this area as special place above our national political authority or national political interests as a designation for the citizenship rights of all human beings -the way in which human beings are entitled to be treated as G'd intended regardless of their national orientation or identity. Now they are saying it with a political understanding and using political language, but essentially it is recognizing the claim of all people to the blessings of that precinct and what it means for the big picture of human entitlement to the human worth and identity G'd made and planned.

Prophet Muhammed, the prayers and the peace be on him, claimed that entitlement to human worth; and in his life, we see it demonstrated under his leadership in Madinah al-Munawwarah -the Illuminated, and also associated with the Sacred House, the Ka'aba at Makkah, the Blessed or al-Mukarramah. That house at Makkah satisfied for Muhammed what the precinct at Jerusalem symbolizes.

This is why Makkah and Madinah, though they are in the modern nation named Saudi Arabia, would never be the capital of that nation. What those blessed precincts represent for the universal rights of man supersede the political interests of any one people. Al-Islam explains that high, special recognition as a tribute to man's dignity both as an individual or with individual human rights, and as a society and rights demanded by individuals in society. Islamic teachings enshrine its respect for the human individual and the human society in these special precincts.

Personally, I am not satisfied that those making the decision to place the American Embassy in Jerusalem are appreciating the argument that it stands for this universal recognition. I don't think that the parties involved representing the state of Israel who insist on this are respecting that this precinct as a symbol is not exclusive to the citizens of Israel. It belongs to the citizens of Israel in the sense of their claim to be respected as a people in community just as it belongs to the Palestinian people in their identical claim. It also belongs to all people who make the claim to human identity and human excellence in community. I believe the American people with a majority of Christians, if they were brought to understand more clearly what principles Muslims see as being preserved there, they would not accept that our Embassy be placed there. Above the political interests our past leaders saw this conflict for placing the Embassy there.

We cannot answer this question without also thinking of the Palestinian people and the potential for them to be further humiliated in their natural desire for dignity and self-determination. The record of history shows them to be victimized by oppressive conditions and the vicious machinery of war and brutality. As with all of the world's oppressed our prayers to Allah for relief and establishment are with them always. I pray also that we do not see desperation and the rise of those who stoke violence and manipulate the innocent lives of the people for selfish aims.

PART I: NATURE AND LANGUAGE

"Surely We have made this (Qur'an) smooth and manageable on your tongue..."

Holy Qur'an 19:97

1   A New Language of Liberty

"Thus, We have made you a community justly balanced, that you may be witnesses for humanity."

Holy Qur'an 2:143

As-Salaam Alaikum. That is Peace be on you. This greeting describes a sacred obligation, and as Muslims we are required to respond with the likeness of it or better. It is important to say that this greeting does not translate "How are you?" The rationale is that if we greet each other with knowledge of the demand to keep the order of peace, we will not have to ask each other what our condition is. The obligation to meet the requirement of this greeting is sufficient to challenge us to present ourselves in the most decent way to each other. We will not have any intention to lie or cheat or misrepresent our intentions if we are conscious of the sacred obligation and contract we are entering into with G'd and each other when we use this blessed greeting.

I would like to begin here with some brief and clear statements of Islamic faith. For us, these convictions are the thinking and expressions of a sacred category of freedom which forms a base for the proper perceptions of human worth and ultimately lead to just establishments in human society. Allah is One G'd, the

1

Lord and Creator. For Him is nothing less than absolute Authority over His Creation, and nothing is or can be joined with Him in His Command. He establishes mankind in knowledge through stages of development and comprehension of the meanings of His Oneness, and how that knowledge best applies and witnesses to human life and human society.

We witness that nothing deserves our obedience in worship except the One G'd, the Lord-Creator. We witness that Muhammed is His Messenger. The highest salute of respect to a human being we ask for and upon Muhammed. He was deserving to receive G'd's Revelation because of his excellent human display even before Revelation. He had a model human life even before his Mission as Prophet among people who were living a corrupted perception of human life in society. The Prophet's innocent nature resisted that corruption in his society, and he did not ignore the pull that his nature had on his rational mind. His mind obeyed the excellence and purity in his nature, and he separated himself from the ignorance around him, and G'd Revealed to him.

We are not inclined to separate our story as a Muslim people in America from the Prophet of Islam's story and tradition. We see strong similarities. In resisting the errors in the Nation of Islam teaching, our late leader, W. Deen Mohammed, was obeying his nature in a similar way. His nature was reaching for clarity concerning the Nation of Islam's teaching on G'd, and man in society. His moral urge and sensitivity brought him first to the contemplation of systems in the natural world, and then to the Revealed Knowledge given to Muhammed, to satisfy and answer the demands in his nature. That clarity that was given to Imam W. Deen Mohammed and that is responsible for his knowledge is a salvation for Muhammed the Prophet's following in the modern world. We say this with firm knowledge. It is at the core of our origins and destiny as a people. It is our language.

The world now is following too much in the way that the Enemy of man wants. Most people in this world unwittingly follow the influences of the Enemy of man. *'Enemy of man'* is precise language. It is not interpretive or metaphorical. The Satan or Shaytan, as the word is given in the Holy Qur'an, is a thinking, a mind, patterns of reasoning that want to disrupt the life that G'd planned for man to choose as his best and most suitable choice of a life for himself. Any conscious or strategic behavior resulting from life-choices that intend to disrupt the human natural path toward human excellence is the strategy and influence of an enemy. This is Allah's definition of an enemy to man, not my definition. The Shaytan's influence gets past most people's conscious minds because much of man's society is built from his movements against man. Most people accept society as it is. They are not seeing themselves as fit to challenge its direction. They just 'go with the flow' as the language goes in the tongue of the Schemer and his followers.

But, there is always an informed minority standing and leading and opposing the schemes of the Enemy. Both the oppression of the people and their liberty is in language. The enemies of man manipulate the world's language usages. But, it is in Allah's Plan to stand man up with the clarity of language, the Clear Book, and the Book living. The Book living is Muhammed the Prophet, the highest salute and the peace be upon him. His wife said that his life, his character, that which he ordered his life upon, was the Qur'an. And so Muhammed is a living body of knowledge and language. The best teachers in Islamic knowledge understood this, and we are the followers of the great Muslim reformer of this age, Imam W. Deen Mohammed. He taught us this.

This is a very special time we are living in. It is described as the time of the new earth and the new heavens. This description is from Scripture preceding the Holy Qur'an, and also from a specific Holy Qur'an teaching. This language is addressing what modern man now readily identifies as global influences that manifest in a new thinking and new behaviors; new realities of knowledge in use to introduce new systems of order that regulate and influence human life and choices everywhere in the international world. No spaces in the world are untouched. There is a sacred category of freedom that assists mankind in this time. It is not any freedom. It is a special freedom that has its own word in the English language and its own meaning in the American understanding. I am not pursuing the American or English meaning of the word necessarily, but it is important to say that this concept in freedom has been and can continue to be corrupted. I am distinguishing the idea of freedom given in Islamic teaching as a component of man's natural inclination to be respected in society. The demand in the nature of man to have freedom of opportunity and freedom of selection to choose and pursue the best life for himself is the sacred category of freedom called *'liberty.'* Islamic teaching presents liberty as one of the wombs for human progress.

I have chosen the word *'liberty'* carefully here. Not all freedom, or *just any type of freedom*, is desired by people ordering their lives in the disciplines of obedience to G'd. Liberty is a sacred property of freedom. Freedom to think and act should not be the only way we understand freedom. In America, at the invitation of the language of the commercial establishment and the nod of hidden powers, the people are influenced to act on their freedom as only a function of impulse. They do not want you to think. They just want you to act, and impulsively buy whatever they are selling, or digest whatever is presented to you. Americans, and even most within the reach of the industrialized or technology-driven world, are directed by this seduction of external and subliminal stimuli. American media programming and other deadly spiders hiding in the world-wide-web can capture and poison you by displaying every freakish existence there is, broadcasting through the airwaves every example of impulse-driven, unconscious, undisciplined human behavior. This is a corrupted liberty, and is not the Islamic moral interest in freedom.

The Islamic moral interest is a true liberty -the freedom to acquire knowledge, to think, to act, and to make informed choices for moral and principled achievements. Liberty is a higher order of freedom. Those who restrict sacred liberty are in the category that should be opposed and resisted. Those who corrupt liberty are devils seeking control of man's ability to make moral choices.

Muhammed the Prophet made demands of his society in Makkah to respect his rational choice of the Oneness of G'd and to respect the common dignity of human life. The leaders of Makkah rejected that liberty. They oppressed the Prophet by attempting to force his and his followers' compliance to the Makkan Chiefs' designations for what should be worshipped and what class of people should be respected and should have the rights of moral choice. Bilal, a slave of Makkah from the black Habashi people of Africa, did not have the rights of moral choice under the Makkan system in pre-Islam Arabia. Neither did most women have this natural liberty, nor any class of persons that were not acknowledged by the Makkan tribal hierarchy system of rule. Pre-Islam Arabia did not accept the idea that all human beings are entitled to public rights or the respect of dignity by nature. The Prophet's teaching was pro-actively identifying and aiming to protect the properties of natural liberty, and from that womb of this liberty came the great Islam-influenced change in human society. This is why Muhammed the Prophet is known as Liberator.

I am referring to liberty as the choice of freedom from the darkness of artificial fear, and the choice of freedom from the darkness of ignorance. Ignorance is darkness, or the rational mind inclining toward and succumbing to darkness; and artificial fears are the shadowy, dancing delusions that further frighten the rational intellect from taking in-hand the responsibility of reason, and reaching to confidently claim the dignity of reasonable choices.

It is necessary for the healthy and natural progressions in human development, in the human psyche, in the human soul, to consciously and aggressively separate from ignorance and its influence. Its influence can lead to an artificial or irrational fear, which in turn transforms into burdens and obstructions to progress.

A sensitive and compelling urge, or spirit, operating within or as a property of the human nature, can and will detect mistreatment, and it will alarm the nature, and the nature will summon the intellect to rise against an oppressive darkness. This is also the process for an initiation in the intellect of man to appreciate and recognize the light of knowledge. The Qur'an instructs that the Prophet's example and his teaching are light, and that we are to claim the path that it illuminates, obeying and following the disciplines of that path. True light then, is liberty. Light is liberty from ignorance, oppression, and artificial fear.

In the United States we have a national symbol in the Statue of Liberty. In the hand of the Lady Liberty statue is a lighted torch and at her feet are broken chains. The statue stands resolutely in the river, breaking the shackles of oppression with the sole (soul) of her feet, while holding the light aloft to guide herself and her followers out of the darkness. It is a guiding light for the human spiritual nature which finds itself in the murky, troubled waters of an intellect which cannot discern clearly because of a blindness brought on by the darkness of irrational fears. But the spirit has a compelling effect on the nature, and it instructs the nature that there is more than the darkness. The light is fueled and manifests because the spirit has been authorized to use *true* fear as a teacher to awaken the nature. The awakening is light, and the nature senses it is being oppressed. Then the nature moves in the direction of a new sense of freedom and demands change. With the new light energy, it feeds its intellect with the logic necessary to break the code of its shackles. This is the natural order for resisting oppression. It develops in the processes of nature and the straining in the intellect. The spirit moving the nature makes a path for the intellect to establish and fortify systems of liberty. Systems of liberty lead to civilization. Liberty is a womb for civilization. Allah planned for human life to find its natural liberty, and establish itself with liberty in this way. This is a spiritual language. But, we know that we have not been created for only a spiritual reality or destiny. There would be no need for us to have a flesh body if what Allah intended was only spiritual in nature. Our life is not intended to be only expressed in spirit. G'd created us from material and in a material reality. What we construct from our material reality acts to display the health and strength of our spiritual origin, understanding and commitments. In optimum health we function as both a healthy spiritual and material body. With our material body using material language in a material earth, there are many instances where our spiritual knowledge will not be clearly understood or even welcome. In many circumstances our spiritual language will not translate with an audience unfamiliar with it. It takes high skill to communicate spiritual truth into understandable material expressions. However, our material presence is a major factor for introducing our spiritual orientation. If we are healthy materially then that suggests we have an intact spiritual constitution. America's material strength, or any nation for that matter, points to the power of its fundamental spiritual premises.

If a body is not healthy materially, or not growing as a material body is intended to grow in a human community form, then it would be proper to analyze its spiritual health in diagnosing the cause for the more outward or obvious problem of what is lacking in a human individual or in a human community's material existence. Under-developed nations and peoples are said to be in a third-world existence. They are not developed materially, and not acknowledged or respected spiritually as other nations or peoples not in that category. They exist in a third reality. I am not adopting this language for myself. I am pointing to it. This third-category existence of human life is the condition that comes about as the result of an extended period of oppression or the onslaught of moral decay and ignorance. It is not a part of man's nature to be in this condition perpetually. No matter the outward forces that may be orchestrating and reigning over third-world realities, this condition is not acceptable in the soul of a true human being. The stirrings and natural processes initiating the urge for expression will demand the avenues of liberty. Monumental spiritual and material rejuvenations come as a result of the nature and spirit seeing and embracing liberty.

Our faith informs our choices. Islam gives the clearest and most direct path to discovery and uses of man's natural and sacred liberty. We do not have to choose the prevailing political language, or commercial language, or the language of nationalism, or of some false race-narrative to define or distinguish us. Islamic teaching authorizes only the clearest language to address any oppressive circumstances that challenge man. Systems of relief from trouble are derived from a basic appreciation and understanding that man is created to be free. Muslims in their correct consciousness -the consciousness that G'd created them with and for, need not borrow from the language of communism or capitalism. Those aspects within these ideologies which speak to man's inherent claim on the properties of freedom are evolved out of nature. Mankind is designed upon the universal Design, and therefore what is in him that connects with what is around him is intended for his development in the Plan of The Designer, *Al-Faatir*, as G'd is referred to in the Holy Qur'an. Therefore, we cannot take from the racists and the supremacists and their idea of the human design. Neither does the Holy Qur'an incite us to violent revolutions or rebellions against the order of society. Muhammed the Prophet's teaching points to useful knowledge in all universal systems of knowledge that the Lord-Creator-Designer intended as lawful, honorable, respecting mates for human nature. The mating of the human intellect with the order of the natural world brings man to a spiritual awareness that feeds and fosters his healthy human development.

We, the Muslims of African-American descent in the following of Imam W. Deen Mohammed do not seek to distinguish ourselves in any way other than as G'd Guides and Wills. We want to be acknowledged as a community of faith in G'd. We do not accept to be defined as a political body or an ethnic body or an economic body or even a religious body, only. Islamic life is all of these and more. It is a well-established fact that many informed and intelligent people strongly reject organized religion and they resist its influence. They also reject much of the language of the political and economic world. Most of them are not atheists or anarchists. They are intelligent human beings, and they recognize from facts of history that these so-called religious, political, and economic bodies have denied the rights and disrespected the intelligence of the masses of human beings. They recognize that many speaking in the name of religion have oppressed, exploited, and dominated mankind through the use of religion and myth. So, when we say we are Muslims, we want to speak clearly that we are seeking our natural urge for establishment in an informed Islamic life by the use of knowledge that is derived from what G'd has revealed as light for all mankind. Our language for this is that Muhammed is G'd's Messenger and Prophet, and that the message revealed to him is light and guidance for all those who desire to govern themselves under the intelligent disciplines of G'd's Authority.

We believe that G'd has brought favor upon us. We are the people from Africa that were separated from the nurturing supports and provisions designated for all humans in their human social identity due to the abuses inherent to American slavery and its associated systems. We are the people characterized by a corrupted misreading of the Bible and Christian teaching as cursed by nature, black. We are the people surviving a construct derived from the false sciences of social and economic Darwinism -ideas which declare that there is always a class of human beings to be rejected, abused, and denied, to deliberately justify our oppression. The attempts to weaken the African-American soul are documented. They were designed by this society and executed against our human innocence with a surgical precision. These plots to weaken us continue, in a measure, by consequence of our own failings and neglect to perceive and address our condition effectively, and by the intended structural devices that breed residual injustices. But, if we conclude that G'd entitles man to a dignified existence on this earth, then we must also conclude that G'd has permitted this suffering, that He planned our difficulties, so as to establish us in spite of the evil scheme against us. Shaped from oppression and born from the womb of the sacred urge for liberty, this process has made way for a new human mind and a new human language to develop within the unique language environment of these United States of America. We are a new human community not seen before on this earth. We conclude then that G'd has planned our existence and formed us as a people for His purpose. We conclude then that the Muslim-African-American people exist to correct and qualify the uses of sacred liberty for the benefit of all people. We conclude then that we are a new human creation with a message and leadership for humanity.

2   Poisoning the Wheat Harvest

"Or do those in whose hearts there is a disease think that Allah will not make known their malicious resentfulness? Had We willed We could have exposed them to you, then you would recognize them by their names (and behaviors), but you will recognize them by the emphasis of their speech..."

Holy Qur'an 47:29-30

Praise be to Allah. The praise is for Him, and our obedience is to Him. He cares for His creation especially His human creation with the most loving care, even in a quality greater than the most loving and responsible parent. We are not His children but we are His creation. We witness that He is One without any joining Him in His Rule and Command, or legitimately competing with Him. Wherever there are those who believe they can rise to compete with G'd, or they intend to rival Him in some way, they are illegitimate. We witness that He is the Lord and Creator, and for Him is the Creation and the Command. We witness with knowledge that all life depends upon Him and His Mercy. He is the Merciful Benefactor, the Merciful Redeemer.

He has missioned human beings and inspired them to teach humanity what is the best path and the best life. He has created man, men and women, with a nature to obey and He has empowered that nature to exercise its highest quality and to find Him, and in finding Him to find well-being and peace. That is al-Islam.

Al-Islam says peace and our greetings are Peace. And we say, As-Salaam Alaikum. Peace be upon all of you. And we pray the choicest favors and blessings upon Muhammed, and the peace. Muhammed is the last of the Prophets, and He is the universal Messenger. He is the Holy Qur'an living, according to the counsel that his wife gave of his character when she was asked about him. Muhammed is our eternal Imam, our leader for all times. He is the Imam of all of the righteous Imams. Our love and obedience are for Allah and for His Messenger, Muhammed, the son of Abdullah, from Makkah on the Arabian Peninsula.

I believe that we must also say and be prepared to defend the fact that we have been taught correctly in America of the true character of al-Islam. We are not in need of any fundamental instructions about Islamic life or an Islamic life in community.

We have what is needed to further our Islamic life in America and to build great institutions that bear advanced Islamic knowledge for the benefit of America and the world. We say this, I say this, because we are products of the language environment and leadership culture of the Imam of al-Islam, W. Deen Mohammed.

We say he is of the great reformers and perhaps the learned will acknowledge the Times and they will see him as the one guided and expected. If they do then it is good for all Muslims who follow them. If they do not, we know who he is and we will follow and defend his way for as long as we have breath and the ability to think, and we pass that commitment to our children and their children. Those who think this way are leaders among us. We, who are leaders, are not artificial, nor weak, nor afraid. We are obligated to follow and obey the most excellent ones among us, and we follow Imam W. Deen Mohammed with urgency and confidence. And we pray Allah's Mercy on him.

And we pray for the preservation of his knowledge and language, and the continuity of his people. Allah says in the Holy Qur'an of Prophet Muhammed, "We have not sent you except as a Mercy to all the Systems of Knowledge." Do you know that Muhammed the Prophet holds up the worlds of knowledge?

He is called a "guide and a mercy" as is the Holy Qur'an a guide and a mercy. Muhammed *is* the language of understanding that holds up man's purpose for all times in all places. Muhammed the Prophet *is* language for standing man up, explaining his existence, mating his mind with the created world, and sitting him on the throne of his own nature. Man, with the Muhammed-language and consciousness is trusted by G'd to rule with Guidance.

It has been a hallmark of the learned in al-Islam to teach that Muhammed is the purpose or aim for all Creation. To say that Allah completed and perfected His favor on man and preferred al-Islam for man as the behavioral order and context for his highest expression of life, and that He created everything for this, His Mercy, is also to say that Muhammed the Prophet is the singular human symbol and universal example of mankind evolved upon human nature, not Divine nature, to reach a human completed excellence. This truth is complex, and cannot be appreciated or understood on only one plane of review or consideration. It requires extended reflection and contemplation over the arc of the history of nations and peoples.

It requires focused, disciplined thought immersed in the moral environment of our evolving human consciousness. This consciousness is aided by unidentified and imperceptible agents of spirituality to help guide its awakening and expression in us to eventually solidify and become permanent as learned, rational convictions forming the basis of the teaching of an educated Muslim society in all of its necessary disciplines of knowledge.

It has taken Muslim scholars centuries upon centuries to frame this understanding and teach the concept accurately and

properly. But, in the modern context, it has taken the making of
a new nation (240 years ago) on the earth and the complement of
its radical founding idea of a human equality and universal, irrefutable rights as endowed by the Creator of man to communicate
this concept about Muhammed's importance and its accompanying language.

The idea that all men are created equal was radical at the
time it was introduced by the Founders, and though their concept
was correct, their exercise of this idea bound itself to a hypocritical crisis of their own making. In debasing that founding idea
through a legally-constructed and enforced, systemic, pseudo-sci-
entifically-supported artificial race narrative driven by a supremacist white-G'd-race lie, the very human dignity it promised to all
human beings it denied to a specific people. These people, torn
from African roots to serve America's appetite to impose upon
them a peculiar chattel slave labor and slave identity, and the
processes and systems that formed as a result of this, would manifest as a conflicted, ugly America, but would eventually produce
a new people speaking a new language on the earth.

I am describing a native-born American people but without a
human cultural heritage from which to claim support. A people
made empty by American-style brutality and abuses. A people
surviving only by their inherent sense that a new human life and
mind was developing within them according to G'd's design and
plan. A people chosen by G'd. Yes, a people chosen by G'd. There
would be no way for the moral or rational senses to tolerate such
a slave condition or slave psyche, or the post-slavery reality of a
duplicitous Jim-Crow American-style apartheid, except to understand it as permitted for some purpose under G'd's authority.

Some may read this and say how could G'd permit such a
thing to happen to an innocent people, and they will abandon
faith in G'd. Do you think believers don't wonder the same? I can
tell you that free human minds and souls who seek obedience to

G'd have never tolerated this condition. It is the cultivated and informed trust and love of G'd, and knowing that His attributes of Mercy and Redemption are real that establish clarity and perspective for us. He is the Merciful Benefactor, the Merciful Redeemer, and His Mercy rules His punishment. Understanding the way of G'd restrains the believers in G'd from any unregulated, ugly passions or retaliations. But it is a sober restraint. We do not love our enemies or the enemies of G'd. We love our brothers and sisters in humanity. And we fight the enemies and their schemes with our principled life until the logic of their disbelief is defeated and they become human. Then they are fit for our embrace.

And so, we are speaking of a new people, not known on the earth before. A unique, singular human fusion of the conflict between the radical American democratic idea and the hypocritical American environment, fashioned for G'd's great purpose for humanity. What was forming in this people was protected and ordained, beyond the immoral reach of the destructive white race-supremacist forces reigning all around them.

A people designated to carry a spirit and a mind that would speak in infancy with a biting boldness and pride to the oppressive forces of white-supremacy, and then speak in maturity with uncommon wisdom and instruction to serve and maintain ethical democratic structures. The language was new for the American mind, but inextricably linked to mankind's ancient and enduring struggle to uncover artificial schemes and reveal man's true nature and destiny. It was Muhammed the Prophet's language of man's completed excellence, spoken for the first time into the ears of America, but also spoken with a new eloquence into the conscience of the modern world by a distinctly different tongue from what was familiar from other descendants of slaves.

It was not the cadence of Black Church reasoning. It was the distinguished stature of a new people in America. A native Muslim-American people. With this reasoning it can be argued and defended that the womb of the African-American people, and all of the travails that characterize the qualities of and challenges to the health of that womb, was created and exists to produce this mind and this language for the salvation of man's true image, man's true Life, and man's true purpose on earth.

A new people created to introduce Muhammed, and all that he represents, to the world again.

This is not just ordinary language that comes from human sounds from a human mouth, or ordinary human thoughts directing a human being's pen in recording human knowledge. It is an understanding reflected in cultural, political, military, economic, educational, ethical systems that provides the moral logic for a people to stand up, where history says before they did not have the knowledge to stand. It is the language that explains how G'd, the Lord-Creator, fashioned and planned and evolved man's intellect for discovery and use of the potential in his own material and spiritual reality and reverential use of the external environment from which he came. It is the language that explains that G'd created Adam, our first father, to bring out Muhammed. Adam was created for Muhammed's purpose and leadership. Without Muhammed Adam's designation is not fulfilled. Without Muhammed, Adam is not known. Without Muhammed, Adam is not understood. Without Muhammed's teaching and example, his demonstrative purity and perfection, Adam is a mystery and his nature can be manipulated by those who act in hidden spaces with hidden agendas, and against G'd's plan. From Muhammed we know that Adam's nature as an intellect is requisite for progress. From Muhammed we know that Adam is composite, and that he is potential.

From Muhammed we know that Abraham, our second father, is the great and first teacher of the possibilities of man's mind searching his origin, anticipating his conclusion, and instructing us in how to read the evidence in his observation of the material reality for our human mind's progress. Because of Muhammed we can see Adam in his progression reaching to be Abraham. We have no access to this understanding without Muhammed's language. Human nature and psychology are darkness without Muhammed's teaching.

Man approaches his completion as a creation of G'd through pursuits he makes in his urge to survive. In this survival urge is the initiation of a high, social maturity and social order. Man's hopes for himself as an individual intellect are realized in this social maturity. He strains in his intellect and against the resistance and challenges of his failures and successes in spiritual perception and the realities of the material world to find peace for his society. And Allah says to Muhammed that "man is tried in his good and in his errors...." The Revelation to Muhammed is Muhammed's language and it is to produce a Muhammed-people in conscience, a Muhammed-people in behavior, a Muhammed-people in societal structures, and ultimately a Muhammed-people in language.

And so, we are formed from language, and we are awakened in language, and we progress, and our world is made safe and honorable and arrives at its intended conclusion because of enlightened language. That enlightened language is taught and executed in human communities. And so, we can see that enlightened peoples and nations are formed from their traditions of language. I am getting to the main points, but it is necessary to explain these matters so that what we are facing can be understood in its proper reality.

Imam W. Deen Mohammed, in the first moments of his leadership said to his people, "Man means mind." "Woman means womb of mind." "Words make people." The Holy Qur'an warns that a people can be manipulated to lose "their ability to hear and see." They can lose their ability to function because they lose access to their language environment.

The plot to destroy the language environment of Muhammed the Prophet is an ancient scheme beginning with all plots against his life and leadership. In his day there were constant plots against his physical person, even from those identifying in his following. In the 1450 years since then the plots have taken on an even more sophisticated nature. They can be detected in social, political, cultural and economic dimensions to an extent unfathomed by ancient peoples.

Enormous resources have been deployed in every nation on this earth to wipe out Muhammed the Prophet's leadership and language. This includes so-called Muslim nations. Every single time someone in the world assigns the blame of unjust aggressions against innocent human populations to the followers of Muhammed the Prophet there are major resources in play to magnify and exacerbate the issue. In spite of these plots it is true that Muslim populations continue to grow. But, the quality of knowledge being taught as Islam, and the confusion as to the true report of Islam continues to be a major concern worldwide. It is well known that the terrorists who costume themselves as Muslims relentlessly prey upon the ignorance and desperation of innocent but ignorant Muslim masses further complicating the Islamic language environment.

After the Prophet passed away his companions struggled against these forces in their own private and public perceptions and use of his knowledge. They resisted foreign incursions and trends, and defended against internal plots that attempted to convolute Muhammed's words and deeds, and to even corrupt the Holy Qur'an itself. In their struggles to preserve the Prophet's teaching, his companions -may Allah be pleased with all of them, on occasion mistakenly misread Muhammed's emphasis and the emphases of the Holy Qur'an, cascading over time into major errors and schisms of understanding.

These issues of misunderstanding even now deeply affect the character of Islamic preaching and Muslim relationships within the Muslim reality and non-Muslim reality. The Prophet predicted these circumstances, judging and advising his companions that "at the head of every age will come a Reformer."

These observations are not an unjust or ignorant criticism of the Prophet's companions. It is not to question their sincerity, aptitude, or commitments to the Prophet; nor to discredit their enormous and invaluable contributions to Islamic understanding and the establishment of Islamic community institutions of knowledge and tradition.

It is, however, to identify that the forces that seek to disrupt Islamic life, or we can say, human life in its model form and demonstration, are at work and have been since G'd announced His plan to create a 'khalifa,' or trustee, in and of the earth with a spiritual destiny, a moral nature, and authorization to rule with Guidance in the material reality. Even in the language of their choice for designation of the leaders after the Prophet... the term 'khalifa', the companions made a serious error.

The Prophet, with the words revealed to him in the Holy Qur'an, established 'khalifa' as the term designated for the enlightened, inspired, and guided human community trusted for rule in the earthly order; but his companions came to read it to refer specifically to the rulers 'succeeding' the Prophet. In making the term exclusive to their idea of leadership they incorrectly gave themselves the title G'd fixed for Adam and all his descendants who obey the good human design and nature. In so doing the term was 'corrupted', its understanding 'confused' and 'misplaced' and the door to further troubles in understanding of the Islamic mission was opened.

In a highly regarded report by the Prophet's companion, Ibn Abbas, who was revered for his clear-mindedness and devotion to the Prophet's specific teachings, was asked about a religious community matter. He answered the questioner with the exact words of the Prophet and the questioner went on to comment and insist on what he had heard on that subject from two of the previous 'khalifatain', Abu Bakr and Umar. Ibn Abbas, flabbergasted, looked into the sky and replied: *"I am expecting a storm of punishment to rain down on our heads. I have answered you with what the Messenger of Allah has said and you are telling me what Abu Bakr and Umar said!"*

These kinds of influences crept in among the companions, and while their attention was on matters that they sincerely considered of serious Islamic importance, language began to form among them that would ultimately attempt to threaten the sanctity and security of the idea of Islamic community, understandings in Islamic knowledge, and the purity of the Holy Qur'an itself. Within 30 years of the Prophet's passing the Islamic community leadership, made up of his closest companions, had come face-to-face with major, existential assaults on Islamic life, most having to do with the proper use and understanding of Islamic knowledge and language.

Ten years have passed since the passing of Imam W. Deen Mohammed, and as I have pointed to Islamic history to appeal to the astute and the truthful, his people are now in the midst of a major and existential assault on their language environment. Those of us who were formed by Imam W. Deen Mohammed's knowledge and language, and particularly those who worked closely with him, were sensitive to attacks on his leadership when he was with us. We were at his side, strong and committed, and would not permit such sentiments to gain momentum around or near us without being checked firmly. Over these last 10 years these attacks have been unrelenting, increasing in their ferocity and disrespect and primarily targeting our younger generations-our children and grandchildren.

From the earliest moments in September, 2008 the open belligerence began. The attacks were subtle but unmistakable. In an article written just moments after news of Imam Mohammed's

passing, Imam Zaid Shakir, ostensibly honoring and eulogiz-
ing Imam Mohammed, wrote "...Imam Mohammed will not be
remembered for what he SAID, but what he did." The character
of Imam W. Deen Mohammed's leadership is, if nothing more, all
about what he SAID and DID. The importance of his words, his
language of understanding, cannot be siphoned from his works.
His language informed his works, his leadership, and his people's
understanding.

**But more importantly, his language is correction for the centuries
of misunderstandings that have so adversely affected the disposition of Islamic teaching in the world.**

The problem for the corruption of the knowledge in Islam does
not begin with the abusers or the sinners or the terrorists. It begins
among the so-called learned, the ulema, who in their jealousies, and
their intellectual schemes against what they consider to be a sinful
and undeserving public and a corrupt Muslim and world leadership, have permitted the unleashing of a scourge of ignorance and
terror on unsuspecting publics as their strategy to purge the world
and Muslim life of sin. Most Muslim religious leaders do not want
to accept the truth of this, but there are clear indications that these
scholars they so revere have bartered with the Enemy of man and
his followers.

Imam W. Deen Mohammed saved the Islamic message for
the world, and preserved it with his language in his people and
their commitments and their example as an Islamic community in
America. We are now experiencing the full-on attempts to subvert
the legitimacy of that message and to erase it from the public use
and memory or corrupt its understanding for future generations.

Most of the mosques said to be in the association of Imam W.
Deen Mohammed's following are today not recognizable in terms
of their emphasis in Islamic teaching. One such historic mosque

has even allowed itself to be re-designated 'Nation's Mosque', not during Imam Mohammed's life, but after his passing.

I am told that those who preach at the mosque have been instructed to not emphasize Imam Mohammed's name in the Friday sermons, but to "use his language." Use his language but do not associate it with him. Erase his name. Those are the instructions. Is the Islamic moral confusion and hypocrisy not clear? The mosques in the association of Imam Mohammed's following and the generations of lives reared on his teachings have produced a lively, intelligent, informed, progressive and viable Muslim identity. It is in fact, THE Muslim-American identity, from which pride in Muslim-American life and institutions have been formed.

In other words, there would be no language 'Muslim-American' and no identity 'Muslim-American' and no understanding 'Muslim-American' were it not for Imam W. Deen Mohammed.

And yet, those who are looked upon as important leaders in his community are actively working to erase his name, and ultimately his knowledge and language, from the tongues and minds of the people he raised with his teaching.

A recent article in the New York Times (August 13, 2018) has the headline: "Harlem's Muslim History is 'Being Erased.' She's Trying to Keep it Alive." The story centers around the iconic Malcolm X Shabazz, but there is not one mention in the article of Masjid Malcolm Shabazz or its people.

It makes mention of the following of Louis Farrakhan and Clarence 13X in Harlem, but no indication is given that the original Muhammed's Mosque #7 on 116th and Lenox Avenue established by the Honorable Elijah Muhammed and his following was renamed Masjid Malcolm Shabazz by Imam W. Deen Mohammed when he became leader of the Nation of Islam.

Is this not documented evidence of the attempt at erasure of Imam Mohammed's language environment and people in public view? The addresses Imam W. Deen Mohammed gave over the years at this, one of the most historic landmarks in Harlem, renamed by Imam Mohammed in honor of Malcolm's work there, were central to much of our understanding as Muslims in America. Any who were present during the weeks Imam Mohammed spent there in the 1980's will witness to the impact of those addresses. *Imam W. Deen Mohammed Speaks from Harlem Books 1 and 2 (Challenges That Face Man Today)* in countless ways defined Islamic understanding, and for those who took those teachings seriously, has focused the language and emphasis of Muslim-Americans in Harlem and in America since then.

I have mentioned previously that Imam Mohammed warned his people that there would be efforts made against them with the intent of weakening their loyalty to him and attempting to corrupt what he was teaching them, or redirect them to other influences and emphases in Islamic teaching.

The pursuit of useful knowledge is a requirement and duty for all Muslims. Imam Mohammed respected this commitment and sought to build meaningful relationships with well-meaning Muslims of every continent to become better acquainted with them and their knowledge, and them with us. But the Muslim world has never consistently responded in kind.

In fact, it is clear they are actively funding religious, educational, and charitable initiatives to attract our people's attention and recruiting our knowledge, experience and citizenship advantages, so as to direct its potential for their motives and uses.

Unbeknownst to our people, we are drawn into activities and relationships appearing to be innocent calls for a general Muslim solidarity, only to reveal a process of inquiries and judgments implying that our Muslim-American deficiencies in knowledge and culture need to be redirected to their stores and applications of knowledge to be more authentically Islamic. This has gone on for years, and some of this is ignorance on the part of the perpetrators, motivated by the stereotypical portrayals of Muslim African-Americans in American pop-culture. But behind the ignorance is a hidden hand with motives that are purposely obscured from view.

In this regard Imam Fethullah Gulen of Turkey and his interest in specific individuals from among Imam Mohammed's people is revealing. If he has wholesome and upright intentions toward the people of Imam W. Deen Mohammed, why not make those intentions known publicly, and why not request a meeting between our most responsible leaders so that they may report on the possibilities for such a relationship to our people?

The public and honorable relationship between Imam W. Deen Mohammed and his people and the late, respected lady Chiara Lubich and the Focolare people is an example of the proper manner in which two peoples can communicate and cooperate for humane objectives. We have not seen or been invited to this kind of relationship with any from the Muslim world, at least not in the sense of two peoples working together publicly and in their respective communities to advance humane interests and causes. With some notable exceptions, the attitudes of most of the leaders of immigrant communities of Muslims in America has been more their interest in 'correcting' us than respecting and cooperating with us.

In September and October of this year two conferences have been planned which are taking up the general subject for planning and understanding Muslim life in America. These conferences, in Mississippi and California respectively, share many of the same participants addressing topics which the organizers deem important matters for Muslim history and Islamic life in community as perceived from Muslim-American perspectives.

To the extent that the organizers and participants are noted contributors to answering questions facing Muslim life in America, and they are respected Muslim leaders and thinkers, I believe these conferences can be worthwhile. They definitely both deserve our attention.

I was struck by some common language between them that I am inviting the best students of Imam W. Deen Mohammed to take note of and review. Both of these conferences refer either directly or indirectly to 'shadows' in the life of man ("out of the shadows to the forefront...") - Mississippi Conference; ("from Dusk to Dawn...") - California Conference.

Is something obstructing the organizer's objectives for Muslim life that is casting a shadow they need to address as they progress toward their desired destiny in the West? Or, do the organizers feel there is a need to re-orient us to the East and change the perception of the reality they know is behind Muslim life in America? Our lens for progress in al-Islam in America is also our lens for understanding in Islamic teaching. We have no guided vision for our life as Muslims except that which came from the one designated to show us and teach us Islamic life for the first time in America.

Deviating from Imam W. Deen Mohammed's vision for Muslim life in America spells punishment and destruction. Because of him our shadows are guided, and we are not accepting someone's artificial shadow over us attempting to convince us we have been in the darkness and that we now need their light.

We pray for Allah's Help. We pray for His protection of us in these difficult moments. We pray that He make us to see clearly and make us to be strong against our enemies. We pray for His Mercy on Imam W. Deen Mohammed, and to keep us firm with that which is best for us. We cannot manage this life without Him. We ask Him to make of our lives what He prefers. We ask that we not be permitted to act on our own, but to act only in obedience to Him. We hear Him. We obey Him.

We ask Him to forgive us, and we acknowledge that to Him is the enduring existence. And these are the words of the Holy Qur'an and teaching of Imam W. Deen Mohammed preserving our Life against the plots.

3   The Sacred Entitlements

"What Allah opens out of His Mercy for mankind none can withhold. And what He withholds none can authorize after Him. And He is the Exalted in Power, Perfect in Wisdom."

Holy Qur'an 35:2

As-Salaam Alaikum. That is, Peace be on you, as Muslims greet. Praise be to Allah. And our praise for Allah is based in faith and knowledge. It is an educated and guided and sincere recognition of G'd and His Mercy and Authority. It proceeds from the knowledge of what we have been created in the first instance and what we are created to become according to how Allah planned the human life. And we believe in that plan and we abide by that plan. We are not guessing about it and it is in that plan where we find education to support us in ordering our affairs in the way that is best and most beneficial for our human life. This is what we mean when we say the praise is for Allah. These are not just ritual words with no knowledge to support them. It is our grasp of the knowledge that supports the words we say that earn respect for us as a Muslim people. It shows us to be a Muslim people thinking and building. A people growing upon sound reasoning in our faith. Not blind faith or ignorance.

We witness that nothing is to be worshipped but Allah alone and we witness that Muhammed is His Messenger and His Prophet and His Servant and we should say His Slave but it requires an explanation to those who are not familiar and perhaps cannot perceive the meaning of that without an informed explanation. It is the obligation of the best informed of the teachers of al-Islam to make this explanation to the faithful and the followers, and all people. We pray the choicest blessings on Muhammed and the peace upon him and his companions and all of the truthful and pious followers that include even those approaching our time, this Time in this America.

In this Time, we have experienced a unique set of circumstances. We are now observing and understanding these circumstances to have universal implications as they have unfolded in this America. And so, we see that we have been helped by Allah in a special way because our circumstances were so different and peculiar in this environment and to this environment. That help we received is best seen in the focus and language of our Islamic tradition.

We believe it is a guided tradition and we can support that belief with very strong evidences from the primary and most reliable sources of Islamic knowledge. That guided tradition is expressed in a very special language of Islamic instruction and understanding in Islamic knowledge that does not begin with the schools of traditional Islamic knowledge that are followed throughout the Muslim world. It begins for us with the story of the crushed dignity of an orphaned people whose inherent human nobility was disavowed by America and the world, but restored with a direct help from G'd. It is the story of an orphaned people separated from their mother-land and father-land with no education to nourish their human developmental urges except that which was permitted and fed to them by those who orphaned them.

An oppressed, denied, enslaved people in America, whom G'd saw abused and struggling in the American environment and lost, severed from their connections and continuity as a people from Africa. This history may very well spell out the most damnable of the crimes against the human soul ever known or ever perpetrated. But we are not recalling it to charge an indictment, or for bitterness against those who perpetrated it.

We could devote a lot of time to that specific crime, and we could lecture the white race on their crimes against this people over hundreds of years even up to this present America. We could include how they introduced their race as the image of G'd and used the sacred essence of Scripture to justify their trade in the human flesh and souls of this people. We could directly relate how the profits from this abominable trade created their dramatic rise in material dominance throughout the world and how the rationale for pursuit of more wealth and control contributed to a sick reasoning that justified for them the wholesale destruction of the cultures of indigenous, non-white peoples on every continent of the earth.

We could make the argument so well that the present-day purveyors of that reasoning and the beneficiaries of that trade would have no alternative but to plead guilty in the court of universal justice with all non-white peoples of the earth standing ready as witnesses for the prosecution. We have the truth, proof and knowledge to do it. But that is not our purpose today. Too many a great mind has been taken off the task of focusing on the needs for our living human destiny by wading too long and for no good reason in that pool of pain and tears.

What we want to point out is that within the context of that historical crucible a new people were born in America without the support of any spiritual or cultural father or mother. I repeat, a new people were born on this earth, on this continent, in this land without a father or mother!

So, we acknowledge these circumstances in America, this America, and we see it as witnessing to the planning of G'd for the purpose of reintroducing to the world an improved and renewed human awareness and Islamic thinking. A new mind brought into the world through a new people who were once Muslims in Africa, to be applied in a new world and a new society. We witness that this new time meets the qualifications for what enlightened souls have pointed to as the time of the great Redemption. And the leader in this Time, the one who labeled it in the best and clearest language is the Guided-Reformer, Imam W. Deen Mohammed. Imam Mohammed labeled it the Day of Religion. He called this time the Day of Religion. And we witness that he is the Guided-Reformer, and those that accept him follow the guided path of knowledge, understanding, and application. And this is well-known and expected among the learned scholars in al-Islam no matter the school of thought they belong to. And this is our firm witness based in sound knowledge and clear proofs without conjecture or guess-work.

We intend this address to reach the general public, not only the Muslim public, and so we greet the Christians and others. But especially the Christians who may be reading this and who are celebrating this the day they call Easter.

We want all of the people of faith in this land we are citizens in to know of our plans and that our plans include an honorable respect for them in their religious and community identity, and our plan for ourselves respects their plans for themselves. We are thinking of the Islamic teachings of Jesus the Christ, as he is named in the Qur'an, and his mother, Maryam, upon them be the peace.

We have Qur'an-Arabic expressions that are most comfortable for and familiar for Muslims, but we are speaking today in the public spaces and so we are using the language most familiar and inviting to the public. Muslims who cannot be patient with this should be more attentive and obedient to the Islamic teachings and requirements for Islamic Call.

Your Islam is not exclusive, it is inclusive and includes recognition of those who are named in our Qur'an and are central figures in the serious and productive life of others who are not identifying with Islam as their faith. Sane Muslims know that Christians and Jews and any serious people wanting for themselves and all others the honorable life G'd planned for human beings are not the enemies of each other. The Qur'an says we are drawn together in this earth, and so it is a demand upon us to live and prosper together.

Jesus is called the Christ as it is given from a Greek word, and the Qur'an says that his mother was chosen above all the worlds or all the nations. In fact, there is a chapter or Surah of the Qur'an named for her and another one named for her family or environment of faith. We see this as speaking to her pure and obedient nature and its complementing social environment. One description of al-Islam is the religion seeing the human nature and the natural world as complementing each other, and the one attracted to the other in its objective beauty and purpose.

Mary, the mother of Christ Jesus, is presented in al-Islam as of the highest and purest human nature, the perfectly obedient nature, the nature in its best form. And her story is presenting the role of that nature in its perfect, obedient state that has been prepared by G'd for His enlightenment and guidance, and to build what He intends upon it. And He builds upon that perfect, obedient nature so that it benefits from His Mercy. So, Mary is a representation for the function and purposes for that nature in society.

This is one of the descriptions for the first standing, the first breath, the first lifetime of the human existence. It is given in the Qur'an also with the description of our first father Adam who was standing upon that excellence in his nature before G'd breathed into him, and with Prophet Muhammed when the Qur'an says, *"and you have lived already a lifetime among them."* That first excellent *"lifetime among them"* qualified him for his role in establishing the society G'd wants for human beings. That nature is necessary as a foundation to begin the processes for what comes next. That which is built upon that nature cannot come until that nature has been established and is functioning. And what comes next? What is the consequence of that functioning nature? It is the rise and development of the intellect that eventually meets with the Divine guidance that directs it so that it may build and establish the Life, the promised Life, the good Life in society. And that is what we are introducing today, or I should say re-introducing.

For ten years our people have been methodically losing their connection to this language and appeal and knowledge. But it is not all of your fault. Our enemies put us to sleep, and I know that, even if you who sleep do not know that. So, I am required to use mercy in waking you. We awaken the sleeper with the true call, not by an alarm. We don't startle the sleeper, but we don't whisper either. This call is distinguishable from other calls. You may be called to what is referred to as al-Islam but it may not awaken you from your slumber. You may continue to slumber in another language environment that destroys your natural dignity just as slavery did and think you are a righteous Muslim. No, this call is to you to be free and responsible. It is clear and firm, and just. It is also kind. Today and forward I mean to deliver it to you in the name of Imam W. Deen Mohammed and with his methods, his language, and upon the authority of his guided path.

So here we have the first of the sacred entitlements that I would like to discuss with you today. That is the entitlement to the benefits of our own nature, our own pure, human nature.

When this address is concluded I feel confident that you will appreciate more how respecting this entitlement for its full value will provide us a powerful platform for advancing our life in this America and for helping this America with its struggle to find and define a healthy patriotism again. We cannot support an unhealthy patriotism. Our good nature cannot swallow it. Our good nature will throw it up. No healthy people will stay healthy long if their idea of their worth and purpose has been corrupted and becomes separated from the design and purpose in their G'd-given nature. The first teachers of the American idea understood the promise and potential in the G'd-given nature. They referred to it with great respect and wanted to guarantee that this land, its people, and its government recognize that no ambitions for their American idea would be possible without a profound, thoughtful respect for it. It is true that they were slave-owners and slave-traders but they knew their sin. And they warned the republic they were building that that sin must be addressed or it will mean the destruction of the society they hoped to be established.

There is a lesson to be taught to this America from Muhammed the Prophet on the treatment of slaves and captives. This America would do itself well to see and to study what the true report of al-Islam says in addressing the rights and the supports that are due to oppressed peoples. I say the true report of al-Islam.

And where will this America get the true report? It can be heard from the humane and informed preachers of al-Islam who come from any of the nations who have Islamic heritage. But it can be heard best from the people I described earlier—the people of Imam W. Deen Mohammed.

And so, the founders of the American idea saw the great potential in the nature—that if it were trusted and liberated and respected properly it could develop to become a society enabling and sustaining levels of human brilliance and productivity not known before. The founders knew also that there were dimensions to human possibilities for maintaining society and that it could not develop properly without a connection to the Creator, or Judge, or Supreme Authority. Those dimensions are best identified in what Allah has revealed in His Guidance to mankind.

For this society to endure in the picture that the founders had for it, it cannot rely only on the decisions of justices of the Supreme Court in interpreting the Constitution; or the elected officials in the Congress or the occupant of the White House. It cannot rely only on the powerful commercial interests, even though all of these are necessary and all of them should be conscious of it. The founders identified that the Republic cannot endure and will not endure except that it finds complement and compliance with what the nature demands of respect.

The general citizenry must have an accurate perception of that entitlement and it must look to those who are best acquainted with what G'd has revealed to assist man's intellect and to direct it properly in respecting the inherent demands of the nature. That has historically been addressed by the religious establishment. But even there we have seen increasing acts of intolerance and ignorance.

There is an obvious breakdown in that perception in the common people, and there are clear signs that basic decency, and the quality, elementary, common relations even on the local community level and between neighbors has been on a rapid and steady decline. Basic, fundamental, structural bonds have been and are being pulled apart. It is in the political language. It is in the behavior and choices of law enforcement in their widely documented aggression against young, black males throughout this America. It is in the influences from media which actively and daily manipulate the public's trust in leaders.

Those who in the population of this America understand that a fresh look is needed at our bonding ideas and principles comprehend well what is at stake. If these structural bonds are not repaired, we will see in plain view and real-time the destruction of the American idea and the essential bonds of the American people. Some of you might say that is exactly what we are looking at now. I don't disagree; however, I know that Muslims in their right understanding are not permitted to flee difficult circumstances without making a strong effort to improve them.

Every ethnic group in America is entitled by nature to develop their own idea of community that best serves their inherent right for social, educational, economic and cultural establishment. That entitlement cannot be dominated by another people. We have the dignity of citizenship rights and laws to defend that dignity and those rights. Islam teaches that every newborn, by his or her birth, makes an undeniable, free and unobstructed claim to the human identity. Even a child born with deformities or retardation of their mental ability are absolutely entitled to the acknowledgment and respect of their humanity. These facts are well-known by the people acquainted with Revealed knowledge. Muhammed the Prophet said that every child is born upon the nature. Society under that influence obligates itself to therefore respect the human life and its inherent rights and entitlements.

America's immigration policy once invited and guaranteed opportunity to any human being from any place on the earth, to enjoy not the blessings of America as such, but the blessings of liberty defended by the American idea of respect for the human nature. America will not survive as an all-white nation inviting immigration from only white nations. There may be language to support this notion and movements to this end from persons motivated by language coming from high places. But America as an idea does not support the notion that whites are the only race entitled to human respect.

How we measure the meaning of our bonding-language, our patriotism, and what we understand to be a healthy patriotism is something that the religious establishment must examine and contribute to. All people of the religious knowledge and faith traditions must speak more clearly to respecting the human nature entitlements in the context of improving our perception of patriotism. Our healthy patriotism based in a reevaluation of the founding principles is our redemption.

I am a leader among Muslims representing a learned tradition of Muslims in America. Whether the majority of Muslims recognize me or not, I am obligated by my devotions and my knowledge to contribute to the strengthening of the bonds between peoples in my society. I do not deny that in that process there will be misunderstandings or conflict. But the Qur'an and Muhammed the Prophet's teachings do not show me a picture of human society without problems. It shows me what human beings are entitled to and it makes a demand of me to work to see that those entitlements are responded to properly. That is our struggle. That is our jihad. To be a patriot in this America is to work for the salvation of its founding premises and clarity about them. If no others have an attachment to that but the followers of Imam W. Deen Mohammed, then it is we who have been chosen to lead America to its redemption. That would not be unexpected. We have certainly been prepared. However, I believe that calling attention to respect for the fundamental human life and the plan for that life that we see clearly designated in Islamic teachings using this language will be an important factor for helping others see the same from their own stores of knowledge and perspective. And if we Muslims will speak that specific language of patriotism into the ears of all Americans this healing medicine will course through the veins of the society.

We do not believe that the heart of America is damaged, it is her thinking. We can reach her thinking and this emphasis on a different perspective of patriotism introduced into the veins will rise to the heart and through the arteries reach the brain. We are drawn to the heart of America, not only as its seat of emotions, but its seat and hub of intelligent sensitivities.

Muhammed the Prophet was attracted to the ancient center of religious faith for the Arabs, but it had been thoroughly corrupted from its original purpose. He never worshipped the idols deposited there and rejected all behaviors that defiled its sanctity even before he was missioned as G'd's Messenger. It was upon the original meaning and importance of that ancient shrine or House at Makkah as the Qur'an describes it, that was established with Adam and then Abraham, upon them be peace, that Muhammed ascended. He ascended upon the recognition of its first meaning, the meaning established before ignorance and selfishness and materialism as symbolized in idols crept in. He sensed its true meaning as the hub of mankind's highest nature, that which connects all humans to each other and obligates them in their best behaviors and thinking.

He ascended upon that recognition and G'd showed and taught him, enlightened him of the important lessons of the farthest mosque at Jerusalem. This is from the teaching in the Qur'an. And G'd invited him to the highest reality, the highest expression and perception for the human soul and he brought that knowledge from that experience as a mercy to his people for the establishment of human life in society as G'd intended and planned.

And this is the second great entitlement. The second great entitlement is that human beings have a right to an honorable life in society.

We intend to address more concerning these two entitlements in future addresses. But for now, it is important to focus on the first one in the context of improving our sense of unity as citizens in this America. If we accept the American citizenship then as people obeying Islamic teachings, we are also accepting responsibility to serve the best possible life for all citizens.

In a sense we ascend to greater roles of responsibility the more clearly we perceive the central idea that organizes us as a people within a national or citizenship identity. If America had no realizable destiny for Bilalians (African-Americans) then the majority of us would have left its citizenship. A few of our people have done that because they were so hurt and offended by the public language and behavior of disrespect for our humanity through the years from slavery and the cultural arrogance of the white race in its structural and institutional defiance preventing us the very basic franchises of citizenship, that they could not allow their souls to perceive that any good life could be enjoyed in America for them. I don't think any self-respecting Bilalian in America knowing its history has not at one time or another considered the possibility of leaving America.

The followers of the Honorable Elijah Mohammed concluded that there must be at the very least a mental and spiritual separation and exodus, if not for anything but sanity as a potential citizen. There is no way to serve the society thinking as an inferior. The Honorable Elijah Mohammed and his following were the foremost influence for African-Americans in breaking the chains of mental slavery. They outwardly rejected all vestiges of the white world's attempt to dominate their lives and cast out all language to describe their worth given them by the white world.

When I refer to mental slavery, I am referring to slavery of the psychological type which was necessary to maintain chattel slavery and continues today in many forms. One of its forms is the lie of race supremacy—that one, particular race has been exclusively entitled to the blessings of human identity and therefore an absolute right to control and manage all resources of the earth. Too many of our people are still slaves in this way and to these influences. They believe they are free but their choices and behavior say they are slaves to the oppressor's view of their worth.

The author of all lies that distort the true picture of humanity and human nature is the Chief of the oppressors. That crime cannot be charged only to dupes or followers or victims. I am speaking now of the one who rejected and deceived Adam and refused

G'd's plan for him when G'd announced his creation as the one to be trusted with the rule of society.

Patriotism, the language of bonding, is in our hands to help reform this America. If we look carefully at our religious teachings, we will see the honor and respect G'd pays to His human creation and we will also see the obligation on us to share our perception. No one will oppose our commitment to this but a devil or an ignorant fool.

In proclaiming our recognition of the original promises of the founders and demonstrating our enlightened understanding of it by pointing to what our religion promotes, we have a most significant and timely role in this America and the world.

An America with a corrected language of patriotism protects our bonds as Americans-the bonds across only imaginary boundaries, and displays to the world watching that these ideas are worthy of belief and support.

The New America lives in the language of a new patriotism. That new patriotism respects the dignity of human beings above territory or wealth or political messaging or political advantage. It pays tribute to human culture in all decent expressions. It is in fact the true human culture and it comes in every intelligent language and respects every intelligent humane demand. It values the roles of men and women without exclusivity and supports the nature-based importance of masculinity and femininity. It is the only salvation.

We pray G'd's continued favor and protection on all people—those whose lives are comfortable and those whose lives are not. We pray that He strengthens us to increase the effectiveness of our work for addressing the human dignity in this America, improving our perception of patriotism and its language, so that it helps our society here and so that it is help to all human beings struggling for common human respect and attention in this world. We pray always for Allah's help and guidance.

Part II: NATIONS AND JUST SOCIETY

*"... those saved from the stinginess and avarice
of their own souls, they are the ones to achieve
success."*

Holy Qur'an 64:16

4   War on Innocence

"... and do not treat us with injustice, but direct us to the path of balance."

Holy Qur'an: 38:22

As-Salaam Alaikum. That is Peace upon your individual and community self. It is our greeting and commitment, and it is also the name for G'd. It is a major and meaningful matter that G'd authorizes us to use His Name in our greetings. *As-Salaam* is one of G'd's Names according to our Holy Book. So, our identity as Muslims says peace. The religion revealed for perfectly guiding that life and completing that identity, al-Islam, also says Peace. Our greeting is Peace. And the G'd Who missioned His Messenger Muhammed to teach humanity all of this, His Name is *As-Salaam* which means the Origin, and the Owner, of Peace.

The praise is for Him. We acknowledge that we are His creation and His servants, and that we owe Him our conscious obedience. We believe in Him and that none has more love and care for our human lives than Him, not even in comparison with the love of a father and mother for their children. He has planned our human life that it prevails in excellence above and beyond plots against it. And that even our failures are in His plan to aid us in turning to Him and turning to the power in our natural potential for dignity and progress. We believe that He revealed His Message and sent Messengers to demonstrate the life as He intended. And Muhammed, the prayers and the peace be on him, is the universal Messenger and a Mercy to all that is created and exists anywhere in G'd's vast and immeasurable Creation. We salute our Prophet Muhammed with the highest salute, and further, we are obligated to follow and obey him, and we are obligated to follow and obey those most excellent ones who established themselves upon his teachings and example. Among those righteous souls is the Imam of al-Islam and leader of a great Muslim following in America, Warithuddin Mohammed. May Allah grant him the Mercy.

We are near the day of the great celebration and significance for the people of this, our land of birth and/or citizenship, our homeland; and I would like to say more about what I perceive as our heritage as native Americans coming from the following of Imam W. Deen Mohammed, but I think our people may not understand it fully coming in this form of public address. At least, not yet.

The people will have to hear it in my voice and see it in my face to know it is truly the Earl Abdulmalik Mohammed named by Imam W. Deen Mohammed as his Representative associated with the words before many of them will accept it. And that is as it should be. We are as native to this land as are those referred to as 'Native Americans.'

July 4th is our American national observance recognizing the birth of these United States as an independent nation among the nations of the world, independent in the sense of having its own national identity and valuing and relying upon its own citizenry and its own idea of a national destiny for its citizens within the family of nations in this world. Nature entitles that kind of independent pursuit of excellence, even in the expression and aspirations of nationhood.

If we see America in the concept of one people entitled to that destiny and striving together for a "more perfect union" as the Constitution's opening statement says, or we may say *"a more perfect oneness"*, then we can see readily how the idea of this nation and the destiny perceived for it by its Founders is evolved out of a recognition of this natural or nature-based entitlement. The continuity and potential of the people are aligned with the 'oneness' the Founders perceived in human nature as a shared property living in all individuals and groups of humans, and worthy of acknowledgment and demanding a suitable environment for development. That is the ideal of a democratic republic in America.

Peoples looking at America and risking their lives to get to America, this is what they see that is so much worth the risk of dangerous travel to escape the injustices of where they are. They are fleeing lands that will not recognize or protect this sacred human innocence, and they believe that America can and will. Trouble in America does not come with them that desire that "perfect union." Trouble starts when the principle in nature upholding the ideal is not obeyed, or where the principle becomes corrupted and falls away from its original focus.

Trouble also comes when American leadership and institutions suited in the rich traditions and language of American freedom and justice, refuse to acknowledge its founding principles, and instead allow the unleashing of devilish forces and influences of assault upon the vulnerability of that innocence. If America is not already at this precipice, it is painfully close.

There have been many serious abuses in the context of this nation's story that are a far distance from what Nature entitles human beings to and prepares them to achieve. That is acknowledged, and some of it is unforgivable, or I should say in a category above any human capacity to forgive. Slavery and its associated abuses, the dominance of the white race in all of its systems and faces of oppression, of their African-American property-posses-sions spreading over centuries in various forms, that used G'd's Name and G'd's Word to undergird and justify itself, is not for-givable by a human soul. It was a crime against G'd and against His innocent and defenseless human creation. It was a sin that could only be forgiven by G'd, too complex for any one person to fathom, too diabolical for even a whole white ruling class to repent the evil of it, too devastating for a whole race of black people to forgive.

We believe, that is, many African-Americans and certainly those of the people of our Islamic history and tradition that begins with Mr. W. D. Fard and is settled with Imam W. Deen Mohammed, that G'd directly intervened in this affair and set the patterns and language and understanding to permit a correction and a redemption. It was too much for the mind of the African-American people to think on forgiveness. Too much wholesale pain and horror. It was too heavy a burden to carry in the human heart, and the human heart can carry great burdens.

Even for the whole of the American people it was just too awful a sin for any act of National repentance to reconcile the injustice. Only G'd's Favor on us as a people and a Nation, with His Mercy, could have saved the African-American soul from that condition, and saved this, of the mightiest nations in human history, from the potential destruction created by that singular evil and ugliness. That is a story we will soberly tell over and again for our children and their children, in order to preserve the proud beginning legacy and special destiny of our Muslim people in America.

We teach our young people that the context of our human awakening in America has not been without extreme difficulty. But, built into that difficulty and struggle has come a high regard and sophisticated, detailed recognition of the productive prop-erties of human innocence. This is a shared recognition amongst the most spiritually sensitive of the peoples associated with religion-inspired faith, and a property belonging to all Americans. It is however, a special and matured sensitivity in the Muslim-American people of Imam W. Deen Mohammed.

Today, we announce our intent and determinations to point to the principles that strengthen us to defend that innocence again and again. Even in view of a public outcry against our American domestic political leadership, we are not influenced to turn away from the powerful psychology which supports our citizenship commitments, and our healthy, informed Muslim-American patriotism. This is our native home, and we will have the life it promises!

Those who have come from a certain experience have more of the obligation to identify the threat when it manifests or attempts to manifest. There have been no people fighting the influence of the devil in every aspect of his assault on man's life more than what is shown in the record of public Muslim spiritual, intellectual and cultural disciplines in every age since the time of Muhammed the Prophet, the prayers and the peace be on him. We share this with Christians and Jews and others referred to in our Holy Qur'an as 'the People of the Book.' It means they are a people following disciplines in which they seek G'd's approval and support, just as Muslims are supposed to.

The people of Imam W. Deen Mohammed are from a tradition of Islamic understanding and social courage that will not allow us to be at ease when our homeland is fraught with a prevailing spirit of divisiveness. We are in our peace and we build upon our peace, but what we desire and have for ourselves we want for all others who deserve it. The heart-wrenching wrongs and immoral abuse of family prosecutions, child and infant detention, and family separation supported by American legal institutions and policies at our border with Mexico, targeting primarily Christian immigrants fleeing inhumane treatment, is deeply felt. It is felt by American Jews whose families were destroyed by holocaust Nazi Germany but found their way to Ellis Island and American struggle, opportunity and establishment. It is felt by American Christians, the offspring of war-fatigued European refugees who rebuilt families by way of the benefits of American citizenship. It is felt most especially by the descendants of chattel slaves, who have no recall of the faces that were torn from Africa because the humanity of their slave families did not rise high enough in the estimation of slave owners and traders to be respected as human families or souls. This is the ugly face of the War on Innocence.

One very serious and very important and very productive Imam in our association mentioned to me recently that he was participating on a panel discussion where he was emphasizing the importance of education in our dawah or work to invite the public to see al-Islam and Islamic community aspirations correctly. He said that one of the other participants who is recognized as a scholar in al-Islam differed with him and wanted to offer some inferior reasoning for his different opinion.

I thought to myself that whatever body bestowed that title of scholar on him, if they are worthy, they should revoke it publicly. I doubt they are a worthy Islamic body if they produced someone and stood behind or accepted someone with that mind. I don't know of any subject in Islamic teaching or the Holy Qur'an that gets more support and attention than thinking, education, and the processes of thinking and education.

I said to that Imam that I would have said "I seek protection with Allah from the rejected enemy Shaytan." But this matter speaks to the point. The enemy of man wants disruption in these natural processes by which G'd teaches us and cares for us through His teaching and evolves us continually toward an increased and increasing excellence. The Enemy wants to confuse and interfere with these processes.

There is no more important or powerful change-maker in the behavior of any people, than exercising the ability to think. And more specifically, thinking on G'd. Not thinking on G'd in G'd's nature. We have no legitimacy in that thinking. It is an offensive notion to go too far in attempting to see into G'd's nature. Thinking on G'd is a guided affair for us. G'd put it in our nature to find Him so that we should obey Him. He says that we are created to be His servants or for His worship which in the Arabic language comes from the word that means 'service.' Our identity as G'd's servant means that He has put into our nature the need to find the One to whom we owe our obedience. That is the highest of our thinking. When we find the truest of ourselves then we have found the self that He has made everything for. And the domain and benefits for our thinking is in all He has created - "a garden that is the expanse of the skies and the earth." He has given us a universal environment and made it subject to us in order to grow into with our minds, utilizing all of what it yields of knowledge for our material and moral advances.

And that is the meaning of the 4th, or the 40th year of full strength, or 40 years of wandering, or the 40 days of trial by water, or the 4 winds that raise the dead bones, or the 4 rivers that feed the development, or the 4 mountains of stability, or the 4 birds of training, or the 4 wives from which to realize a righteous future by care for the neglected human identity, or the 4 principles for (mate) selection, or the 4 gardens of reward, or the description of Professor W. F. Muhammed as WD-40, or his introduction of his mission on July 4, 1930, or the only Temple built from the earthen mud (ground) under the Honorable Elijah Muhammed's term of leadership - Muhammed's Temple of Islam #4 in Washington, D.C. America is born on the 4th and in this evolution of man's nature wherein he becomes conscious of his own purpose and destiny. It is all speaking to the same principle.

It is given in the Holy Qur'an that mankind was once one community. And the verse says that that unity was dissipated by human contentiousness and human diversity. The word in Arabic suggest differences, but not just any differences. The Qur'an is not simplistic language. It is language of the most profound meanings and depth of meanings. So, the word that is describing differences is hinting toward understanding the properties of leadership and acceptance of responsibility in man's nature.

The differences are concerning the disposition of man's mind in how human life is to be carried forward as human society. The verse in the Qur'an I am referring to goes on to say that the problem for mankind's unity was reconciled by a 'Word'.

This is a very strong emphasis on mankind's 'oneness' coming from the Holy Qur'an. And I am of the belief that this is the principle of 'perfect union' that the Founding Fathers saw as the American destiny. Maybe they perceived it in other Scriptures that carry the same line of instructional purity, or maybe they saw it in the Qur'an. I am not wanting to make that point at this time. Certainly, we know that at least Thomas Jefferson took a keen interest in revealed knowledge; and we know he had a translation of the Holy Qur'an in his library.

The important point here is that what is given in revealed knowledge confirms what is already in Nature. The orientation that mankind begins as a species upon this principle of unity, or 'Word,' is a powerful urge for the development of social philosophy and social dynamics, ideas which are applied to address man's social aspirations.

The idea of democracy as social philosophy evolves upon a recognition of this original principle and identification of man as one community entitled to a specific type of quality existence.

And then we see also in the Holy Qur'an that G'd says, "This, your community, is one, and I am your Lord, therefore worship only Me." So, here again is the association between the unity of man and the Lord of man Who evolves man upon the support of a natural inclination to hear and obey that Lord. So, from this principle we can arrive at the notion that man has certain favors or rights conferred upon him by his Lord, that man's continuity as a social community is related to how he has been evolved by His Creator.

Man's highest possible progression as a species comes in the context of the realization that his human origin is fashioned upon 'one' original design and that original design also functions as a predicate base for his community. He has been created to evolve upon this design, and the destiny or guarantee of the design is human community in its best form. This is the 'Word,' the central, overarching principle that reconciles man's contentiousness and diversity. All of this comes out of his original purity or his original innocence. The principle manifests also in the Holy Qur'an language that says the "skies and the earth were once one entity..."

This language forms the basis for a powerful psychology that is continually working for us as Muslim-Americans. Our determination is to see that the American idea works for us, Muslim-Americans, and all people desiring it. This is America's guarantee.

As I said, we are native to this land. Our claim to its promises came as lessons in G'd's school of redemptive authority. Our tradition begins with a summary rejection of America in its abuses, and in its authority over the destiny of African-American lives. In the estimation of the first teachers of the Lost-Found Temples of Islam in the Wilderness of North America, the white race lost all of its credibility as a civilized race. Whites were referred to in its language as a race of devils, snakes, and skunks of the planet, with no inherent ability to adjust their thinking or behavior. We are the people who because we were conscious of what our people endured at the hands of whites in a degree of sensitivity more profound than most in our race, we accepted and embraced the idea that a new psychology and language environment was needed to heal us.

The community, or people, of Imam W. Deen Mohammed are proof of G'd's Merciful Two Hands acting upon the affairs of this country. Imam W. Deen Mohammed upon ascending to the leadership of his father's Nation of Islam explained that while his father knew instinctively that African-Americans had to reject the white man's dominance in their lives and thus completely separate from American spiritual and psychological influences, his leadership beginning in 1975 would set us upon a system of language and understanding enabling us to re-enter America as a new people, with a new mind and a new patriotism.

Our plan for our Muslim life in America is squarely reconciled with the American idea in its purity, in its innocence, and our plan recognizes a place in America for all who are similarly reconciled. The test of its purity as truth is whether its benefits apply to one group at the cost or to the exclusion of another, and whether the institutions which uphold the democracy obey this purity.

That is why when human beings, men, women, children -families from Central America are presenting themselves at the United States border seeking the recognition of this society, the reason their situation resonates with us is that we see that what is driving them are natural human properties, properties of the nature-based human innocence. It is in us and them to want safety, shelter, access to provisions. It is in us and them to desire better, and to build upon that desire and develop upon that desire.

When G'd says that our human community is one and that He is our Lord and to worship Him, it means that our nature He created us with entitles us to whatever He created, and also that we recognize the responsibility to work for that entitlement in such a way that it can be universally realized.

The Founders of this society wanted to guarantee that entitlement as a life of dignity to all who could see it. The whole premise of their idea of American society was built on respecting the natural innocence of the sacred human person that is equally accessible to all human persons. The question as to whether America and its institutions should be rejected because it has violated the purity of its democratic promises was answered by Imam W. Deen Mohammed and his people in 1975. We know well that American leadership can be and has been duplicitous.

The Founders themselves had the problem of these contradictions, and because of these contradictions the pure idea ultimately became threatened by a serious rational and moral corruption. The Civil War, no matter what historians may say about its causes, state's authority verses federal authority and such, was the conflict exposing America's hypocritical contradictions. The American society at that time could not make its grand claims of respect for the human dignity and deny that same dignity to a particular people. The contradictions resulted as a revolt in the life of the society. The toxin of hypocrisy was too much to the American national organism, and the system itself threw it up.

To the extent that America cannot or will not see this, it will incur an exacting, terrible price. But we are here! Thank G'd, Imam W. Deen Mohammed's people are here! This is our native land, we will not see it be destroyed, and our reasoning and logic lives and speaks. Just as this nation was tested before, lessons in G'd's school of redemptive authority are delivered, explained, and administered again by us, though the devil hates it.

And our language, our mind, and our patriotism are its redemption again. For those of the people of Imam W. Deen Mohammed, if your Islamic senses are serving you properly in his tradition then you will be moved to confidently take what I am saying here and share it with as broad an audience as possible.

And you will find strength in these words and the determinations and understanding that has formed them.

You will put aside any inferior reasoning and support what is clear and certain in service to G'd to help this nation and its people find their way again.

5 Crisis in Muslim Leadership

"Allah establishes an Example: a city enjoying trust-security and comfort-satisfaction: It is supplied in abundance from all of its establishments; yet it was ungrateful for the favors of Allah: So, Allah made it taste of extreme hunger and extreme fear as if confined in a restrictive garment, because of what they committed themselves to."

Holy Qur'an 16:112

As-Salaam Alaikum. That is Peace be upon you. And we have given many of the important meanings of this greeting and we continue to express it in its great depth of meaning. We desire that when we speak it and hear it that we recognize its invitation to obey the intelligent disciplines of Islamic life. We invite the Believers in G'd to learn more and appreciate more of our most important and regular teachings. Much knowledge is held in these habits we have that are also teachings in and of themselves.

We witness that nothing deserves our worship or is to be worshiped except the Lord, Cherisher, the Creator of all that exists. He is the Merciful Benefactor and the Merciful Redeemer and loves and cares for His creations, and highest and most cherished of them is the human creation. The Day of Religion, wherein no human soul will escape the reward or the punishment of Justice, is under His Sole Authority. He, Alone, has missioned the Messengers and Prophets. They are His creation and we witness that Muhammed is the seal of the Prophets and the universal Messenger, upon him be the blessings conveyed in the highest words of salute and the peace. He is our leader in all times and for all time. He is the Imam of all of the righteous Imams.

And we witness that the Imam in Muhammed's following who taught us this reasoning was a guided soul and a reformer of this age and were it not for him then the truth and best report of al-Islam would not have reached the former slaves in America or the world as we know it. That is the Imam of al-Islam, W. Deen Mohammed. And we confirm this truth with knowledge.

Greetings to the Muslims in this blessed month of Ramadan. In it is forgiveness, guidance, and mercy for those who observe it in its obligations and practices. As the Muslims in America struggle forward in pursuit of an Islamic community destiny, we carry with us aspirations for improvements for the lives and conditions of all Muslims and the world of Muslims.

We must think and are thinking of the condition of Prophet Muhammed's following in the world and the general state of affairs for our collective Muslim life, our collective consciousness as Muslims. We must have a correct perception of Islamic group identity. Muslims have fixed group aspirations that should define our choices and behavior. We are reminded of these especially in this month of fasting and reflection.

We do not judge the Muslim world but we carry a heavy weight on our minds and hearts about its character and its grasp and attachment to knowledge of the best possible Islamic life and existence. This is not merely an intellectual problem. It is a crisis of emphasis and conflict in the Muslim group spirit. The reality is that Muslims are, generally speaking, a very far distance from the Muslim life taught and demonstrated by Muhammed the Prophet. This is the reality everywhere Muslims are, in Muslim nations where their rule is long-established, and in non-Muslim nations where Muslims are a minority. The disposition of Muslim life is troubled, not at peace. The problem is difficult and burdensome on the psyche of Muslims.

The Muslim world is in a centuries-long denial about its true state. It is has allowed itself to be characterized in confrontation with Western progress rather than in the context of what originally characterized Muslim progress and how Islam came to be respected in the world. That which brought the attention and respect of the world to Islam is not displayed in the present public character of leadership in Muslim lands.

Our brothers and sisters may not accept our perspective, and I would understand that it is painful to hear and know. Understanding what the group disposition should be is more the responsibility of leadership. The quality of Muslim leadership in the world is very poor primarily because it has been in a mode of reacting to the challenging and harsh circumstances associated with the history of colonization of their lands by Western powers.

Rather than planning a healthy Islamic progress in the context of studying and answering the score of spiritual, social, and material concerns that require better solutions with Islamic remedies, Muslim world leadership has adopted policies of pretense to placate the West at the expense of true Islamic freedom, justice, and equality. I am not offering this line of reasoning as if I am a social or political science authority with any knowledge above the experts on these kinds of issues.

Often, we are made to feel that because we may not have an advanced university degree in some particular discipline that we cannot offer a common-sense view that may be even better applicable than the summaries of many of the experts. This is a common criticism directed toward the people of faith that was revealed over 1400 years ago to Muhammed the Prophet to warn the believers to not be moved by this kind of criticism of our perspective so as to limit the influence in the world of what G'd has commanded and its reach to the people who need it.

Many so-called 'experts' have confused a clear understanding of the essential issues with flowery discourses. I am speaking as a believer in G'd and one who strives hard to know and obey the disciplines for decent human thinking and decent human behavior that have been revealed by G'd in the religion of al-Islam. I am speaking as a follower of Muhammed the Prophet and his public advocacy for protecting the inherent honor of all human beings and demonstrating proper human behavior even under abuse and injustice.

I am speaking as a student of Imam W. Deen Mohammed who gave us the best language and applications of correct Islamic understanding and practice as we witness these issues in today's world and how to deal with them. I am speaking as one who has grown into a maturity of that understanding, and now observes even more clearly the Islamic responsibility we have to project the proper and informed view of Islamic teachings.

I am an educated and an informed Muslim-believer with the clarity of truth on my side and the tutored skill to direct that truth toward the falsehoods that hurt Muslim progress and muddy the image of al-Islam. We stand firmly in the school of Imam W. Deen Mohammed's tradition when we look closely at these concerns and alert our brothers and friends to what we perceive.

The criticizers and experts will have to step aside when the sum total of what they offer is incorrect or misguided. The Muslim soul registers and broadcasts that our Muslim group spirit is not anywhere near its best form, and the answers must come from basic, common-sense Islamic understanding.

I have seen recently a photograph taken of world leaders from Western lands and Muslim lands, proudly standing together, with their hands spread upon and across a globe of the earth. Were they grasping each other's hands in the interests of mutual peace, recognition, and security?

Were their eyes and arms meeting and embracing each other in a message of sincere and planned attention to addressing the needs of the world's populations? I did not see that. To the contrary, their hands were strategically locked on areas of the globe, grabbing at a symbol of the earth and its resources. That photo moved me as a conscious display of arrogance, projecting the most distasteful image of ungoverned power, and making the very strong allusion to a will to dominate the earth.

It is common knowledge among Muslims and believing people, followers and devotees of the heavenly religions, that there is no power or authority above G'd in His rule of all He has created. And yet it can be no wonder then, that with Muslim leaders in charge of lands to whom the common Muslim people look for Islamic guidance, showing their designs on the earth with such insolence and impunity, that the group conscience of Muslims is in such confusion, disarray, and desperation. It is no wonder that the poor and defenseless of one Muslim country die as victims of bombing campaigns from a proxy war of those they thought were Muslim neighbors and brothers.

What possible prospects for clarity of an Islamic destiny can the Syrians, Palestinians, Rohingya and Yemeni lay claim to in a Muslim world environment where Muslim leadership is more imitating the airs of the history and degradation of colonial power-interests and power-plays than for the love of human dignity advocated in the teachings of Muhammed the Prophet and the Holy Qur'an? What has happened to take Muslim leadership so far from al-Islam and Muhammed?

And while many in the Muslim world leadership openly turn from the most basic of humanitarian principles which are founded upon universal Islamic interests, the modern Israeli state continues its brazen aggression in the notorious and menacing spirit and force of occupying, militaristic Nazi-Germany.

The Israeli state and its interlocutors make bold claims to a several thousand-year-old legacies from G'd and an eternal promise from Him guaranteeing a particular parcel of land to them, while making no claim of responsibility of what is due to Him of the duty of righteous care for His servants who may inhabit that land with them.

With the nod of great world powers, the Israeli state concentrates their Arab subjects in the same manner in which Nazi Germany concentrated their Jewish fathers and mothers during World War II; first in the ethnic ghettos of European capitals under military occupation and dominance, and finally in the holocaust death camps.

With the state of affairs as they are in Gaza, where Palestinian lives have no access to the dignity of citizenship, nor employment, nor recognized claim to resources of land or sea that borders it, all that can be made of the status of Palestinian dignity is that they are an unjustly imprisoned people in a 25 x 5-mile razor wire fenced concentration camp governed by shameless wardens of bitter abuse, and a holocaust policy of degradation, brutality, and raw terror.

This observation of Israeli government behavior does not in any way excuse the immorality of some in the Palestinian leadership who manipulate the desperation of their stateless, defenseless people through the implementation of a strategy that implores the bartering of their innocence in exchange for the news-cycle of international media exposure.

In laying down invaluable, irreplaceable lives at the mercy of the seasoned, aggressive Israeli military war machine they believe they may jar the world's attention. The reality is that it earns little world sympathy and even less world support.

Coming from Islamic guidance this strategy proves even more despicable than the Israeli occupation itself, because its motivations are clearly without respect for, nor understanding of, the sanctity of life which G'd created. G'd's help will not favor such moral confusion. How can Muslims have confidence in such leadership that wagers the innocent lives of their people? As with the Prophet David, upon him be peace, carefully selecting the five perfect stones of principle, and throwing the choicest one at the oppressive force, will truly expose the enemy.

The problem is serious but it is not out of Muslim's reach with G'd's guidance and help. However, it will not be solved by the customary predilections and ritual lip-service. Muslims have not so much strayed from our expressions of faith as we have deviated from the applications of good Islamic sense and violated clear Islamic obligations.

Islamic rituals preserve great knowledge to address human problems. But we observe the rituals with seals and blindness on our ability to correctly perceive their value. We recite Allah's words with humility in our prayers, but is G'd in need of our prayers, or are we?

Guidance is in our recitations of the Holy Qur'an: *"You are the best community brought out for the good of all people."* This is the public authorization and mandate for Muslim interests in the affairs of this world, and they are also the sacred recitations of worship. And again, Allah says: *"Therefore We have made you a balanced community that you will be witnesses to all people."* G'd's clear and direct instruction.

We humbly say to the learned that there is no tradition of violence in al-Islam. There is no license in al-Islam for the rise of a militarist order. Islam preaches defense against aggression, and the rule of justice over oppression, but there is no Islamic teaching that justifies viewing human beings as pawns to coerce, manipulate, and dominate by way of the rise of mighty armies and fixations on military-style rule. Such ideas are the opposite of the Islamic ideal.

There have been great Muslim armies and great Muslim military strategists, yes; but the Islamic character fueling the demand for military preparations and interventions were permitted to exist only to check the threat of injustice; and it readily humbled itself in protection of innocence and to the authority of righteousness.

Again, we repeat, that the words of the Holy Qur'an are not to be relegated to the ceremonies of Islamic ritual worship. They are life-changing instructions and protective guidance from the Lord of all the Systems that bear and adduce Knowledge, preserved for respect in ritual obligations. To the wise that sense this, and the learned that know this, we point them to the words of the Holy Qur'an as a correction and a salvation for the faulty attitudes in Muslim world leadership:

"O Allah, Owner of all Power and Rule. You give Power to whom You please, and you strip off Power from who you please. You empower with Honor whom You please and You humble whom You please. In Your hand is all Good. Surely, You have authority and choice over all."

We pray to G'd that we see our enemies as G'd has identified and characterized them, and that we see ourselves more clearly and correctly.

6   Salvation for America

"Assuredly, you have in the Messenger of G'd a most excellent, beautiful standard of conduct for any who seek for G'd and the Last Day, and who think on G'd often."

Holy Qur'an 33:21

As-Salaam Alaikum, we greet you our honorable audience. That is 'Peace be on you.' We are grateful to G'd for any opportunity to address our Muslim and American publics, and we are aware that these words are reaching an international audience in increasing numbers.

Praise be to Allah. We witness that there is nothing to be worshipped but Him. This is a part of our public declaration as Muslims. They are powerful words conveying a powerful concept. It means that it is incorrect for an individual to think or for a society to establish systems that promote the idea that humanity progresses by its own merits and abilities without assistance from G'd. If we say that we are responsible for all that has been provided for our development as human beings we are not being truthful, or we are confused, or we have been duped by an oppressor who wants to take our life for his purpose. G'd says that our human creation and progress is a sign. A sign of what? A sign that

G'd is responsible and that we need Him to understand how we are to direct our human lives. We may not give G'd credit but that does not mean He does not deserve the credit. If we are not giving Him credit then we are deficient in knowledge.

Social philosophies may be obstructing our thinking, or man's achievements in science and technology may be clouding our perceptions, and we will incorrectly see man as completely responsible for his own progress. But the logic and reality of our own human development shows us that the new human baby cannot survive without the care of others. And so, we can reason that there is a caring Lord-Creator who has planned the human life and its destiny. When our minds come clear we will follow our natural inclination that He put in us to find Him. And in finding Him we see that He had already found us. And this is one of His names, *Al-Waajid*, The Finder. He has put in us a nature to find ourselves, and in finding our true nature we find Him to Whom we should devote ourselves. The Prophet of Islam, Muhammed, the prayers and the peace be on him, said that when you find your true self you find your Lord.

So, we witness that nothing deserves our obedience above or except our Lord-Creator and that He has no partners to share responsibility for His Rule of His Creation. He supports it without any assistance from anything thought or spoken of as a god, or anything in His Creation. We witness that Muhammed is His Messenger. We ask the choicest favor and blessings on Muhammed and the peace. We follow him and he has taught that we should also follow those who are best in their understanding in the life that he demonstrated. He demonstrated man's highest excellence and performance in terms of moral reasoning and the essential foundations to realize the highest expressions of human behavior. The great teachers of his way after him are in a direct line extending to even this time. And so, we further say that we are the people of Imam W. Deen Mohammed. And we say that

Imam W. Deen Mohammed, the son of the Honorable Elijah Muhammad and Clara Evans Muhammad, was in that direct line of the Prophet's successive leaders in Islamic excellence, and that he was guided and that he was the Reformer in these times. May Allah grant Him the Mercy.

Islam prepares us for a life in community. It guides our sensitivities for community. It disciplines our focus and our determinations for community. Our ritual Islamic prayers are a sign that holds great knowledge instructing us in how we are to order our individual and community interests. Individual prayers are essential and are highly regarded and rewarded, but their highest recognition and rewards are in the context of community aspirations. Prophet Muhammed taught that prayers in the congregation are of a significantly higher obligation than individual prayers. This lesson is not only spiritual in its meanings. In other words, we will have our individual interests and skills but their real worth is in what way they serve the progress of the whole life of the people. Our prayers are not intended to only guarantee an individual's qualifications for Allah's reward. This is not the way we are to see the value of prayer in Islamic teaching. Our recitations in our formal prayer -called 'salat', were revealed to Muhammed the Prophet which he shared publicly. The recitation of the Qur'an is very often a private affair but it always has far-reaching public importance. It shapes the public behavior and conscience of the individual Believer. It shapes our family and community relationships. It shapes our trustworthiness for public service. The best advice we give to one another that is given in the Holy Qur'an is to be regardful of G'd. To be regardful of G'd, or some translator will say "to fear G'd"; but in what context and for what purpose? We would not have references to understand the importance of these teachings were they not shared publicly by Muhammed the Prophet.

Everything we know of Islamic teaching we know from the public community demonstration of Muslim life. So, our regard for G'd cannot be demonstrated in its fullness or in its completion in the private prayer space of the individual. It must be expressed as public principle for the direction of prayer groups, then neighborhoods in prayer, then peoples in prayer, then whole nations in prayer. And Allah says in the Holy Qur'an that nations have failed because they left their obligations of prayer. It means that the people devoted to the guidance have not fulfilled their place in the public of the nation. The nation has become lost because those charged with leadership to invite them and lead them with the most beneficial appointments have been obstructed, or have been neglectful, and thereby the whole people falter and fail, and put the nation's continued prosperity or existence at risk. Our practice of Islamic life, by its very nature, demands that we be a community of Believers demonstrating a perfect morality of human life-behavior that is disciplined and guided by principles intended to complete human life in a public, plural picture. Therefore, we have an obligation to our neighbors, to our fellow countrymen, to all Americans to provide counsel and leadership at all times. In times of peace and war. In times of favor and difficulty. If we are to be truly characterized as an Islamic community, we cannot diminish this obligation. Islam gives us no path to a secretive Islamic community existence. I certainly understand us to be a community of Muslim-Americans. And so, I ask, who is speaking to America to help her and her people, on behalf of our Islamic tradition and in observing this obligation as Imam W. Deen Mohammed did and in the manner that he would approve in this time of difficulty in America? Who is speaking our language and our message to America? I, and those who stand with me, are.

We do not accept that our part in the responsibility to address the conditions and circumstances facing all Americans is turned over to other communities of Muslims who have not the historical legacy or struggle that we do. All peoples in America have in some way become Americans by struggle and they all understand their contributions to be unique and worthy. This country is over 230 years old as a declared united body or federation of States under the authority of a federal Constitution - a nation founded on a combination of the rule of the people and the rule of law, but the history of the womb that formed us in America is twice as old as that. And as an organized community of Muslims, our life in these United States of America is approaching 100 years. I respect the immigrant communities of Muslims here as peoples, and as Muslim-Americans.

At least during the last decade their plans for Muslim life in America has not considered our position, or our history, except as that of a less legitimate Muslim body. They accept that we believe we are Muslims, but that our Islam is in some way defective. We have a strong history of welcoming all Muslims to America, beginning with students who formed the Muslim Students Associations on college campuses in the 1960's. We have respected, saluted, and contributed to the success of their plans for Islamic life as those college students' interests matured into national Muslim organizations. In return they have neither made it their habit to consult us, nor contribute to our interests in any lasting or meaningful way. In fact, in many instances they have used us to step up and into American life discarding their relationships with us except when the appearance of unity serves their immediate political or economic need. They will find that that is a strategic and moral error on their part.

It is well-known by all Muslims that Islam invites and requires us to consult each other. That act of consultation is an act of faith, and is qualified by an inherent demand for mutual respect. The immigrant communities of Muslims in America still struggle with that respect for us, and they secretly perceive us as their adversaries when it comes to the public representation of Islamic life and values in America. Some among them have even conspired to weaken our national Muslim leadership with the tacit help of language and movements that have declared war on democratic and American ideas of society. Also, too many of them have adopted the view of an ugly America which has ranked our humanity as inferior. I do not expect that they will admit to this, and in fact I am certain they will deny it. I derive no pleasure from saying it publicly because Muslim unity is a high obligation and demand on all of us. The Muslim soul is not in any collective comfort when so many are confused about Islamic life. As Muslims we cannot ever be comfortable allowing the ugly America to dictate our attitudes toward each other. Our influence is with the America the Beautiful. But our Muslim unity must be a dignified, honest, human unity -not a superficial one. It is a unity declared by articles of faith. It is a unity based in the fundamental idea of the unity of G-d and His Creation, that is at the center of our Islamic teaching. A political or economic unity is not what Islamic faith asks for above acknowledgment of our natural human properties. Political and economic cooperation for Muslims comes as a result of identifying human honor in each other first. The pure unity declared by Islam cancels the flawed logic of racism, classism, and sexism.

I am addressing this issue with our Muslim-American brothers not to alarm them but to underscore to us and all Americans that it may be that they read inferiority in us because of our neglect for our community-life responsibilities to insist that we aggressively articulate and pursue our Muslim interests as Americans. This does not explain all of their attitude. It is much more complex than this, but it does highlight the problem where it is plainly visible that our own leaders have neglected to study our needs and the needs of our country, to understand the troubles facing us and all Americans. Most of our leaders have disqualified themselves to render the service of Islamic counsel to our country in this its most serious and critical moment. Imam W. Deen Mohammed made it a point to publicly teach the Islamic code of life that he intended would govern the spirit of our Muslim contributions to America. He said that America is strengthened when we are sharing our best life and aspirations with all Americans. We do not have a secret life or secret aspirations. He had no spirit to criticize America as a nation absent of identifying the moral principle at stake. It was his teaching that when America is wrong that we openly and honorably correct her -not in the interest of ridicule or insensitive chastisement, but out of love for our neighbors and neighborhoods, the land of our birth, and the land to which we devote our energy of labor, and prepare a future way for our children alongside others' children. We have this spirit even with the Honorable Elijah Muhammad who was justifiably brutal in his verbal rebukes of the white supremacist abuses of our humanity, but who simultaneously instructed us that he was working for a day that we would have decent homes and friends in all walks of life in America.

Yes, this is our country of origin. We are a new people taking our racial and ethnic stock from Africa, but we are the most native to this land because it birthed us as a new human creation. Our story did not commence for ourselves as a people in any land but this one. African nations do not and cannot claim us, though some of us want to override our collective soul's urge to see our human destiny in America and claim them. If a conspiracy exists to oppress the black peoples of the earth then by reasoning we cannot expect that the problem is solved only by lamenting the existence of the conspiracy. African-American leaders and social scientists, and others of those who are students of the damage that slavery did to the African-American psyche, are so profoundly hurt that pain has frozen their natural human properties for progress and has become their primary expression. It is a spiritual and mental-health condition where they fantasize everything 'black' and 'African' as a panacea.

We cannot be taken in with this thinking by Africans or American blacks. In order for us to embrace them in more than our history of common circumstances, there must be a recognition in their language of a human destiny, and an indication that they are insisting on being more authentically themselves by freeing themselves from trends in their decision making that bear the distinct mark of colonial and slave masters lording their self-conscious and self-esteem, and dominating their subconscious. For the Muslim-Americans who follow the line of leadership completed with Imam W. Deen Mohammed, we understand that it is in America that we formed as a human creation, and it is here that we must exercise our potential toward a human and Islamic destiny. It was not in Africa, but America that an Islamic-conscience awakened in us and was spoken in new expression and new reality. There is no doubt that we were taken from an Islamic past on the continent of Africa, but the tree of our life does not grow in America as African Muslims. It grows from a genetic memory-seed of Islamic life in Africa that has since sprouted into a new and original Muslim life in America.

We are a new Muslim people in America with new patterns of thinking inspired and directed by Islamic faith and reasoning. A new human creation on the earth demonstrated in the knowledge and language of a new human mind. So, we cannot be complacent in our responsibility to address the nation, to address our American co-workers, friends and neighbors, and leaders, in this important time. We do not neglect this responsibility or entrust it to the political interests and public relations offices of immigrant communities of Muslims; nor do we sit still and acquiesce to the messaging of resurgent 'white-nationalist' sentiments; nor do we accept any excessive public lamentation-spirit of blacks or calls for black unity full of legitimate tears but void of focus and purpose; nor are we manipulated by foreign entities attempting to exacerbate a breach they perceive in the American community ethos; neither do we accept to tether ourselves unconsciously to any pseudo-patriotic messaging in this nation in order to satisfy some entity's requirement of proof that we are Americans.

All of this is beneath our Muslim-American dignity. Our American identity has been earned in honorable struggle, and is a proven quantity. We do not recite the 'pledge of allegiance' in public spaces as a ploy to impress government or to prove our loyalty. Our public, historic record points clearly to our allegiance and the knowledge that has inspired and directed it. Our allegiance to American identity is not cheap and cannot be bought.

Its value is registered everyday by the thousands of Muslim-African-American municipal, state, and federal employees -judges, school teachers, police officers, firemen, health care and social-service workers, chaplains, etc. who have labored for generations honorably and in service for the best conditions for life of all Americans. Those among us who place our allegiance up for auction are the cheapest of hypocrites, willing to fire-sale our Muslim-American dignity for two dollars, a foreigner's robes, or a government badge and a title.

Our message to the intelligence departments of this nation is that we do not accept to be labeled or regimented into the current national politics of an identity-prison, or corralled into a new-fangled ethnic camp that has been prefigured and fabricated by a reactionary and fearful, private -not public, security interest said to represent government. Those who have this mind have identified witting participants among us and recruited them to inject a poison cocktail of ideas into our people -the idea that our mosques should be government-directed or sponsored enterprises. Our mosques are not experimental laboratories and observation zones for those trained in the sciences of social engineering to provoke, study, and report on so as to assuage ill-informed government uncertainties! No indeed! Our mosques are houses of worship where G-d's name is reverenced day and night by the faithful, to be respected as are the faithful congregant-citizens of churches and temples and synagogues that fill this nation and guide its members to what is honorable and decent before G'd. Our people who gather daily in our mosques should be honored as pillars of the true American life. Our mosques do not belong to the nation's political or government establishment. Our mosques are not nation's mosques, owned and designated by government authority. They belong to G'd, His Messenger, and the faithful and they direct themselves in the works of serving the good and healthy conscience of the nation in human society.

If our government or its supporting mechanisms ever wanted to ask us about some issue, we have always made ourselves available to answer, even if the group asking was not initially inclined to share our view. I was a member of a small delegation accompanying Imam W. Deen Mohammed when he met with the conservative public policy think-tank The Heritage Foundation and answered their questions about his representation of Islam in a democracy. Again, a few of us were with him when he addressed the *Forbes* Forum on the nature of his Muslim-American economic philosophy and interests. And upon his instruction and on his behalf, I participated in a U.S. State Department *Voice of America* broadcast to Muslim leaders in Egypt, Sudan, Libya, Bangladesh, and India where I addressed their concerns and questions about how we Muslims lived our lives in America, and how we view our citizenship reality, obligations, and future. These are a very few recollections among countless hundreds of meetings over decades where Imam Mohammed addressed our legitimate Muslim-American place in the public of American life. His perspective does not need to reinterpreted or reworked. It needs only to be acted upon with his knowledge and in his language.

We have always been ready to defend the integrity of our government when it has been deserved, and the integrity of our relationship with it as citizens. We have a long-standing public tradition as morally-conscious, scrupulous, and trustworthy Muslim-Americans. We are free, intelligent, and most of us are incorruptible in our Muslim-American knowledge, language, and identity. We have a clear understanding that we live in a society established upon the principle of rule by consent of an informed public.

It was Imam W. Deen Mohammed, who in the 1970's when patriotism was dying in America, physically picked up the American flag in its symbolic significance and declared a "New World Patriotism Day" in America. And so, our Islamic principle that warns of a nation that fails because it leaves off its proper focus of devotion informs our citizenship. We are a proud, dignified community of believing men and women who do not have a false or superficial love for democratic principles. On the contrary, we have a sincere love for G'd and a knowledgeable Islamic commitment to principles of freedom, justice, and equality. Our tradition of Islamic life has proven worthy through a century of Muslim history and contributions in America including veterans of every war to defend the American homeland.

This nation will not and cannot be all that G'd intends for it without our public Islamic contribution, especially as regards errors it may be making in violating its own core and founding ideas. We have grown up and with America. The Bilalian people and its leadership have never been a people consumed by worry over the residents or policies of the White House. In this instance our concern is the condition of the people confused by inconsistencies in the messaging of the American leaders, that are in need of us to lead with our understanding and language. Americans are searching for their origins as a people in language, and yearning to be in the right. We are a nation struggling through a period of regress.

As Muslims, we are instructed by G'd to spend in prosperity and adversity, in progress and regress. We are living in the time of the forming of the new earth, and the new heavens. This is the language of the Holy Qur'an. The weight of spiritual concepts is heavy and it is intended to be. But it would be a serious miscalculation to ignore or dismiss its truth because the language used to describe the reality is beyond the reach of most. The normal and daily operations of this world -the concepts that are in play that have set the order of the world and its governments for the last 50 years or so, are not typically explained to the masses. It is intentional that the world's masses are left without access to the knowledge of how this world works. Because of technology and the ability to share information rapidly and over great distances more of the common people have access to new streams of knowledge. But that does not mean they have been taught how to read that knowledge for their use and for their benefit. Most of the world's population is illiterate. High literacy among the common people is something the oppressors want to prevent. They are in the business of directing the masses of people for purposes they have determined, and controlling the extent to which the common person will be able to read his Life correctly and benefit from it as G'd intended. So, a high degree of literacy related to human purpose and the ability to read and interpret the Times in which we live so as to make the best use of knowledge and freedom is not in the interest of the oppressors.

I am not speaking of literacy enabling a person to read a daily newspaper or a textbook or a novel. I am not speaking of the level of literacy needed to read the requirements to perform well as an employee. Literacy like this is taught in high schools, colleges, and universities to prepare the populace and the work-force to address labor needs and to encourage study that will advance the nation. It is this literacy that brings benefits to mankind on the most common level. Prophet Muhammed and his best followers over 1450 years have led and contributed to the common people having this kind of literacy, encouraging and leading the engagement of the material world and all of its areas of benefit for human progress.

It is well-known that what the West refers to as the Reformation and later the Industrial Revolution was inspired by the preservations of and contributions to spiritual, material and scientific knowledge as enabled by scholarly and assertive Muslim populations from Arab and African lands that had touched Europe.

But this is not the only level of literacy that was the concern of the Prophet. When the Angel of Revelation presented G'd's Command to Muhammed to "Read" and he responded that he had no ability to read, his character as a decent, productive, trustworthy human being was already known and established. The level of literacy the Prophet was invited to was that level where man is most vulnerable and susceptible to oppression. Material oppression is only the outward symptom of the category of oppression that is the interest of man's open enemy. The knowledge that G'd wanted him to read had less to do with what he already understood about human decency as an individual, and more to do with that which is necessary to construct human society in that decency and with language, so as to empower the human life with knowledge that would sustain its development toward a completed human destiny of excellence, applicable as principles in all times and places by all human communities that had access to it.

This is the literacy that characterizes the power of the human nature in the context of community establishment -the literacy of true human liberation and dignity. This is the type of literacy that frees man from the constraints of all worldly, material masters.

The science of this literacy's understanding and applications is the heritage of the people of Imam W. Deen Mohammed.

I am speaking of the literacy to read how the hidden have ordered and organized the world's knowledge and language for the purposes of sowing illiteracy. What I am pointing to is not a baby-language belonging to a holy-ghost following. And don't think that many populations of Muslims in this world are not under the hypnotic trance of a message that preys on their emotional nature. In the Time of the new earth and the new heavens man is shown clearly his material reality and his spiritual reality, where they are leading him, and whether it is aligned with the destiny G'd created and planned for him. What I am suggesting here requires serious attention and reflection.

There is language in America coming from high places suggesting that the nation is lost to its greatness -that it should be the focus of the nation's collective energies to restore a lost greatness. In other words, the nation must exert itself in all areas of its existence for the purpose of achieving 'greatness.' What is meant by greatness in this messaging is not clearly defined, but it has been branded on the American conscience, and it has been interpreted differently by groups in the United States as well as countries in the international world.

The language is meant to provoke but it does not yield any clear understanding of the intent behind it or how 'greatness' it is to be achieved. Many very serious questions arise from this as to what the American people believe about themselves, their commitments to democracy, or to pursuing some kind of imperial destiny in the world. We should conclude that those who created the language meant it to be ambiguous, and they hide its true meaning and its true uses behind many veils. What is of interest to them is how the American and world population act upon it, or react to it. What is of interest to them is how Americans can be manipulated into behaviors that serve the purposes they have by using this language to narrow the interests of the American people, like the use of blinders and a carrot to direct the attention of a plow-horse. This is why responsible commentators are alerting the American people that these are very serious Times, and the language of public discourse is to be looked at carefully and not to be taken lightly.

For Muslims, we are encouraged to pursue excellence, not greatness. And this pursuit of excellence recognizes other's excellence as well. It can be spoken of as an individual excellence, but is never limited to that, and it is laudable and recognizable wherever it is displayed. Obedience to G'd in excellent works is the public and universal rule of Islam. Excellence in worship. Excellence in behavior. Excellence in works. The relationship between excellence and greatness for us is that we are taught to say Allahu Akbar -that Allah is Greater; that progress is in acknowledging the greatness of G'd and what He has enabled for us to grow upon and into. He created us for honor in excellence, and progress in excellence. Even if we are in regress, it is with the spirit of human excellence that we process our condition and what should be done about it.

Shouldn't we be the ones to teach the American public what is meant by the words "Allahu-Akbar?" To say "Allahu-Akbar" signals the movements in our prayers from one position to another, from one epoch to another, from one degree or level of commitment to another, from one level of progress to another. These changes of positioning in our private and public prayers are repeated through darkness then light then darkness again. Our formal prayers are in part a symbol of the rising and setting of knowledge and its proper uses in human society's progress, or regress. Our changing positions and postures in prayer teach that human society is able to continue progressing even while in a condition of regress, and in the many realms of human life and existence, because our pursuits are focused on excellence in obe-

dience, and we acknowledge in every period of change or adjust-
ment that G'd is Greater, and that G'd's plan is working in man's
best interests. We are reminded through every period of change
-whether adversity or prosperity, that the nation cannot be any
greater than its people's pursuits of obedience in excellence. The
aim of the individual in prayer, and the aim of the individual in
his conscientious works, is for excellence. By reasoning then, the
aim of the nation in prayer, that is, the congregation-the people together, should be excellence. Muhammed the Prophet said
in straight, clear language that "Allah has written excellence for
everything." The Holy Qur'an repeats in many places that man's
created mold is excellence. It is therefore outside of man's nature
to pursue greatness. Human beings have been molded by G'd to
pursue excellence.

If any of us were able to speak with the greatest boxer of all-
time Muhammad Ali and ask him was it his objective to achieve
'greatness,' he would answer no. He would acknowledge that he
was spoken of as "the greatest" but then you would see his true
Islamic conscience display itself, and I am sure he would explain
that greatness belongs to G'd and that his personal pursuit was
always excellence. He was not ever pursuing greatness. He was pursuing excellence as an athlete, excellence as a symbol for oppressed
peoples, excellence as a believer in G'd, excellence as a Muslim-
American citizen, and excellence as a human being. And because
of that pursuit of excellence G'd gave him a very special greatness.

The Enemy of man was pursuing greatness and thought himself 'great' and 'greater' when he rejected man's rule in the earth.
How do we know? When G'd announced His creation of a trustee
to rule in the earth -Adam, and commanded the angels to accept
him and his role, the one who thought himself to be a leader
among the angels refused. The one thinking that he was of the
highest and most admirable qualifications for rule did not accept
the man created from the dust and mud, and fluid, and blood clot

of social bonding and achievements. The reason the Enemy of man gave for rejecting Adam was that his purpose and his construction was of a 'greater' significance than Adam's construction and purpose. He was outside of his own nature when he did that, and he is forever inviting man outside of his nature. The Enemy of man invites man outside of his natural created excellence that G'd chose for him to empower him to fulfill his high, dignified, created purpose. The Enemy wants man to believe that his nature is not sufficient to propel him to a satisfactory or superior existence. The Enemy of man invites the children of Adam to abandon their natural desire for excellence, and makes promises to them that he knows he cannot keep, all in the name of pursuing a delusional greatness.

This is the corrupt invitation to greatness that is confusing our American attention on what was responsible for a past greatness, and crippling any collective future American greatness that can be achieved.

We the people of Imam W. Deen Mohammed invest our best Islamic knowledge in an America in regress and an America in progress. This is why I have taken so much time in this address to show a complete picture of our importance to America and why we cannot neglect speaking our message, or entrust it to others to deliver it properly. Imam W. Deen Mohammed prepared his people for this role in this time in America, and he prepared me to deliver that message in his name and on behalf of his people's American and Islamic destiny. An America in regress searches for its best footing from which to step forward in confidence. Its best footing is the nature-based and universal excellence of its founding promises. The promises that identify humanity in its created excellence, and that invite all people to fulfill that excellence in America. When America sees that clearly again, G'd will preserve its people in that excellence as a great nation that other great nations will embrace.

PART III: ON NATURE AND NATIONS

"They ask: When will be the Day of Religion?"

Holy Qur'an 51:12

7   Nationalism is an Evil

"When it is said to them: 'Do not make trouble in the earth.'
They say: 'We only desire to right the problems.' But no, they are
the ones who make trouble, but their perception is corrupted."

Holy Qur'an 2:11-12

We appreciate this opportunity to address our honorable audience. Peace be on you, as Muslims greet each other, As-Salaam
Alaikum.

The praise is for Allah, Highly Glorified is He. All creation
owes its existence to Him. We witness that nothing is to be worshipped except Him. We praise Him, and He is due no less than
our regardfulness and obedience above any other influence that
may be competing for that. He is Lord of mankind, King of mankind, and G'd of mankind. He is above all rulers in the earth, all
potentates, all kings and queens and princes, all presidents, and
no human creation has any special credits or importance with
Him except those who distinguish themselves in regardfulness of
Him through performance in excellence. To understand this saves
us for our best human performance in whatever country we live
in or we are citizens of. The finest, most dependable, and most
productive citizens in any country are those who order their lives

83

with respect for G'd and human life, and the legitimate and natural processes supporting human dignity and human productivity. This type of citizen saves the nation for civilization and civilized interests. This is who we are as Muslim-Americans, the people of Imam W. Deen Mohammed.

When the nation becomes infected with diseased ideas about its reality and its destiny, it is this citizen that stands to help restore it to its most important principles, and contributes to the beginning of a restoration. This is the history of the fall and restoration of nations. If the nation is moving toward objectives counter to purposes that favor human life in its best form, natural and inspired forces stir in a minority of people -or at least one person, from which understanding, then language, form to speak into the collective human conscience with the intent of honorable service to the people of the nation.

Highly Glorified and Praised is G'd, the Lord and Creator. He missioned Muhammed, a son of the people of the Arabian Peninsula, 1450 years ago as His Messenger. Our Holy Book, the guide for our life in al-Islam and the guide for all G'd-fearing people, was revealed to him and demonstrated by him.

We pray the highest and most blessed salute upon him and the choicest favor, and the Peace, and what follows of the same on his family and his companions -the righteous all of them. They are the righteous because of their commitment to preserve his teaching in their thinking, in their conduct, and in their leadership after him. Were it not for the efforts and sacrifices of the family and companions of the Prophet we would not have Islamic knowledge in a form where it can be studied and applied in this modern world.

The great teachers of Islam, the Reformers and Revivers, we pray Allah's Mercy on all of them. They have appeared from many peoples and in many nations over the 14 centuries since the time of the Prophet. We affirm that the Imam of al-Islam who is the son of Elijah Muhammad, Imam Warithuddin Mohammed, is of these Reformers addressing the peculiar conditions for his people in America.

The impact of moral forces and pressures unique to the social environment formed by the American history and language -markedly different from any influence on human life ever before recorded in world history, prove Imam W. Deen Mohammed to have been a guided leader addressing the needs of a special people formed by that environment. We affirm with knowledge that his understanding and language of Islamic teaching reflects the Guidance intended by G'd to serve humanity through the ongoing works and story of this people. This is indeed the characterization of his language that he approved.

This understanding lives, and is supported by proofs and standards in the Holy Qur'an and Muhammed the Prophet's tradition. His teaching and his people have historic achievements, relevance, and value, but they are not a museum exhibit. In other words, the people of Imam W. Deen Mohammed are not an ancient relic-people without a living body and living leadership. Their purposes and value continue as a people speaking the language of Islamic establishment in America and serving the best human purposes on the earth.

This address today is intended to place in focus major global influences pressuring human life, which taken in their aggregate are having a negative impact on human society. In my opinion these forces are attempting to de-construct and deform human life. In this context I would like to point specifically to language that has been presented to the African-American people, particularly young people.

It is language wanting to organize, rally, and invite African-American young people to adopt attitudes which promote a questionable idea and value for African-American life. It is a suspicious language and I do not accept that it is has been innocently formed in the interest of addressing injustices.

The language "Black Lives Matter" is too similar to the Holy Qur'an language that identifies human origin and the designs which G'd has revealed that have been employed to weaken and defeat it, to dismiss it from our attention. By innocent I am referring to the innocence in the human soul that desires what G'd wants for that soul in human society. I believe that most who are using this language or are identifying with this 'movement' and its ideas are innocent. That is why it is important that they are at least made aware of our concerns so that their use of language is an educated use that has been given the benefits of our language and experiences. We do not want to see them manipulated.

It is necessary and important that our Muslim community -the people of Imam W. Deen Mohammed step forward with his message -our message, that the original human life as G'd created and planned that life, is life in black matter. This is where 'black life matters.' The original human life in its true nature is what deserves honor and respect, and all notions that invite us out of that nature for uses that encourage human beings to contend as warring national, racial, or tribal camps, are the designs of oppressors and destroyers. No members in the African-American community have more credibility to interpret and deal effectively with the poisons of 'nationalism' as a false-promise-ideology of social and community upliftment than us. We know well the power of its appeal and magnetism. And we know well its error and its evil.

The human individual in the family setting is the sacred beginning of human society. Family is the primary construction for the development of human life. The human family is older, more essential as a construct, more fundamental and necessary to human society than is the concept of nation. Nations should not ever be in the activity of weakening or severing family bonds. When we see this, the informed in society know that the society is under a direct assault and in existential danger.

Every problem that has existed and perpetuates in the African-American community is directly related to the destruction of social bonds and familial ties during and immediately after American slavery.

G'd does not say that He formed nations and tribes before He formed the thinking man and a womb as the primary social unit. In fact, man in his fundamental nature and the spiritual, material, and social womb that produces his mind for society is the necessary environment from which a nation or the concept of nation is produced. Our pre-occupation with the notion of national identity above human identity is an influence that wants an opportunity to exploit human identity for purposes other than the purpose G'd designated for it. Absent universal humane influences, the concept of nation is a de-construction of human life. Nations have served great purposes in the development of human life in society, so it is not that I am suggesting that the basic idea of nationhood is bad or wrong.

The idea of nation in the context of realizing human social identity is agreeable to human nature. But the nation concept is not to be the primary focus or the emphasis for human social identity. National pride and identity should serve humane interests. The healthy, upright nation is a nation of healthy, upright citizens. It is not the nation that stands the man up. It is what is in the man essentially that stands the nation up. If a nation, or its self-concept, demands a coerced submission from its population to qualify for citizenship, then the human life in that nation will be at mortal risk to lose its human essence, or have it destroyed.

In other words, if human beings are obstructed from their human potential in the interest of the nation, they are being oppressed. G'd intended that the concept of nation and tribe develop from the advancing needs for human social identity, and He intended that it have weighty influence on human interests and orientations. This is the utility of nationhood or a national identity.

It is a vehicle for increasing and encouraging social education and bonding. It is a vehicle to serve human development and expression. It is a vehicle to support original human purpose. Healthy modern nations guarantee the rights of human decency, respect, and recognition to their citizens. If the nation is not serving human life as it was originated to perform in society, then the nation idea is not serving its purpose. The nation as an acceptable idea in the way of G'd is a nation that acknowledges, confirms, and serves human original purpose -the universal social destiny that all humanity shares. Nations that want to carve out for themselves an identity that refuses a common human social destiny will ultimately not survive.

Allah, The Most High, advises that we review the history of nations and see what is responsible for their fall and destruction. This is why the concept of nationhood as a singular or superior focus for identity -competing with natural human identity with the intent to replace it with national identity, is a mechanism used to distract man from the properties of his nature given to him by G'd, and is a tool of oppression using man for narrow and corrupt interests, and depriving man of his G'd-given potential.

This is not to say that we shouldn't have or want a national identity. G'd made man to function with a healthy national or tribal sense. But, that national sense bows to human dignity if it is to serve G'd's purpose for man. And if that national sense of identity makes war with the sanctity of the human individual sense of dignity it has violated its meaning in the life of human beings.

The problem of nationalism -which for this address I am referring to as the drive and appeal of forces and systems to convert and exploit human life and its natural social dignity, ambitions, and destiny to define itself only in a national context and to pursue interests which abuse or reject the inherent dignity of human beings outside of that national context, is the common ingredient for most of the world's unjust wars and conflicts. The desire for seizing of power through acquisition of lands and resources may appear as the most apparent rallying principle for unjust wars between peoples. But more directly, the appeal to blood-honor, that is, traditions of nations and their people in bitter contention with other nations and their people, and a corrupt notion of racial or ethnic entitlements and destiny, was the most effective call to arms. To make its dubious appeal even more potent and alluring, the nationalist cry and idea has historically mixed itself with claims on the authority of G'd's name in religion.

The Crusades were nothing more than manifest European-Christian nationalist fervor. Four hundred or more years of intermittent wars between Christians and Muslims instigated by the Christian West appealing to nationalist instincts in the name and with the face of religion. The 'Crusaders' were not advancing the interests of Christ's teaching, peace be on the Prophet of G'd. They were advancing the interests of a materialist, imperial vision and nationalist psyche falsely labeling itself a Kingdom for Christ, or Christendom. We do not see in Christendom the principles of Christian love for humanity.

In the interest of truth, we must make the distinction of the fact that the wars were started by those for whom they are named, but that there were very serious human abuses on both sides. However, the very word 'crusader' as historical fact signals the image of indiscriminate violence, plunder, and oppression of innocent human life. In spite of the nostalgic, innocuous use of the word 'crusader' in today's Christian vernacular, we cannot excuse or deny the historical facts of aggression against Muslims, Jews, and others in these wars. This spirit for material dominance evident in the language of the Crusaders and others associated with it fueled centuries of European desire and designs on Muslim peoples and lands throughout North Africa, the Middle East, and Asia.

The call of the Crusades whet the appetite in Europe for world conquests in the name of nations claiming rights to lands and their people for Christ's Kingdom on earth -Christendom. Though this type of nationalist aggression was not ever unopposed, its psychology drove a passion supporting European colonization in every continent, justifying 450 years of a trans-Atlantic economy built upon the trade in human lives from Africa, and the devastation of indigenous peoples and cultures worldwide. After 500 years of colonization and unbridled greed and oppression meted upon nearly all non-white populations the Europeans could reach, the same poisoned fervor turned inward on Europe and resulted in the displacement and destruction of millions of European lives in the World Wars. Eventually the same fervor swept Africa and Asia, and though the efforts at liberation from colonial powers is seen as justification, it has since been proven that liberation movements in Africa and Asia directed by nationalist sentiment have resulted in the rule of brutal and repressive regimes throughout the developing world, and extreme misguidance in the understanding of the teachings of the Messengers of G'd.

History is replete with examples of the mass destructive force of nationalism if we will read it carefully: From the naked oppression of ancient Egypt and expansionist-imperialism of ancient Rome, to the expulsion of Muslims and Jews from Spain and the age of exploration-expansionist-aggression into the 'New World' by Columbus, through to World War I and II and the 'National Catholicism' of Franco's Spain, 'National Socialism' of Hitler's Germany, the 'National Fascism' of Mussolini's Italy, the militarist-expansionist-Zionism of the Israeli state, the imperial folly of Hirohito and national militarist arrogance of Tojo's Japan, to 'the religion is nationality' idea of Mohammed Ali Jinnah's Pakistan, Gamel Abdul-Nasser's United Arab Republic and the universal

Arab state in Egypt and the Ba'athism of Hafez al-Assad of Syria and Saddam Hussein of Iraq, to the incursion of a nationalist Afrikaner white minority apartheid rule on an indigenous black majority in South Africa, and even up to the recent end of dictatorial rule of Robert Mugabe in the African state of Zimbabwe, and countless other examples; 'nationalism' has not ever delivered anything to humanity but false promises of racial-ethnic-national glory at the expense of a systematic de-construction of human life and social bonds designed to extract from that life what is deemed necessary to support the world view and material interests of an elite few. This influence has in recent years spawned the rise of an extremism among Muslims to which the West refers to as 'Islamism' or 'jihadism' or 'Islamic-terrorism', but cannot in any way be distinguished from the same misguided destructive nationalist fervor that drove the logic of the Crusades in Prophet Jesus's name.

I do not wish to disturb the dignity of our Christian or Muslim or Jewish friends, or any of our friends in these nations. What I am describing is not necessarily their sin because nothing is superior to Allah's Plan, and nothing is out of the reach of His Plan. His Plan reaches all G'd-fearing people as a warning of the behavior of the wicked from the past that informs the emergence of powerful language, trends, and movements led by the wicked in the present.

The Holy Qur'an teaching is that Jesus, the son of Mary, is G'd's Messenger and not a man-god with imperial authority in the earth. The Holy Qur'an says that he is a 'Word' given to his mother, and a 'Sign', and a 'Spirit' from G'd, and an 'Example' pointing toward what is essential as fundamental teachings for man to achieve a universal human solidarity in Islamic understanding.

(and to digress for a moment: Whenever I say **"Islamic understanding"** I am referring to the teaching of the Imam of al-Islam,

W. Deen Mohammed, that is recorded in his public addresses and writings and my personal interactions with him over decades as his thinking and commentary on the Qur'an meanings and the teaching of Muhammed the Prophet. I am not ever referring to any unsupported guess-work or theories, or to interpretations coming from other's thinking including scholars in Islam. I respect the Muslim scholars from history and presently, from all lands, and I read and respect their important works, but their opinions do not rank above Imam W. Deen Mohammed's teachings for me.

I do not consult their works for any new knowledge, comparisons, or points of clarification. I study their works and their opinions to understand their teaching as influences on their following and how their following have acted in kind to build Islamic life for themselves. I think it is necessary from time to time that I need to make this point clear. My own knowledge is as a product of Imam W. Deen Mohammed's purpose in the life of the African-American and Muslim-American people. I am not the product of anything other than my family's influence on me and the education they provided and encouraged that included the Honorable Elijah Muhammad's voice, the influences of the American environment, and the Islamic influences that began with the Temples of Islam and is completed in Imam W. Deen Mohammed's teaching.

Therefore, for me, *"Islamic understanding"* is the Holy Qur'an and Muhammed the Prophet's teaching in the knowledge, language, and methods of Imam W. Deen Mohammed).

So, to continue, in Islamic understanding, the mission of Jesus was to identify and point to a universal principle built into and enriching man's nature, that when guided would be the predicate base for leading man to form a just earthly order that reflects the peace G'd shows him in the heavens.

Jesus was not missioned, nor is he presented, as the king or potentate for that earthly order. He identified himself as a servant of G'd pointing to the perfection and peace of the heavenly order, and he is presented as a metaphorical shepherd-guide in the earthly order, addressing the needs of an innocent, G'd-fearing flock.

There is no legitimacy for a nationalist idea in religion except as a corruption and an attempt to dominate and constrict human life and potential. I am certain that political and social scientists and historians will dismiss our assessment and criticisms of 'nationalism.' They will say we are 'dreamers' and that the idea of nation-states is here to stay and that they are a necessary 'evil.' They do not care for or understand the way of G'd. Most of them do not believe in G'd, at least not as we do. G'd instructs us to reject and repel evil, and to push it out of our human thinking. We do not accept evil and we do not negotiate with it.

Therefore, 'nationalism' no matter how appealing it may be, is not legitimate as an ideology for human progress in society for any true followers of Abraham, Moses, Jesus the Christ, or of Muhammed, the Universal Messenger. But there is a construct for human life in society that G'd approves. G'd says that He created man from a thinking and a womb -from a male and female, and that He made them into nations and tribes that they will become acquainted. And that the best of them is that one who is most regardful or conscious or respectful of G'd.

And G'd caused Muhammed to ascend to the seven heavens or seven elevations of man's individual moral, and rational, capacity and development, upon the foundation of his sense for the original and essential meaning of the Sacred House and its black-corner-stone: that the human individual and his life and inherent potential, are sacred; and He made him to see a light in the farthest mosque at Jerusalem and the blessing there: that the sanctity of the human individual must be established in society, yet not only in a tribal reality; and then He brought Muhammed to see al-Madinah, the City, in one night, in one universal Vision, in one universal Promise: that man's destiny in society must respect his individual human properties not only as a tribe, but must cooperate for the collective human enterprise and enfranchisement of human community establishment in one universal human reality. This is the construction of the human world G'd revealed to Muhammed.

The ugly de-constructions of human potential and human nature and human ability made possible because of the rise of nationalism continues to this very moment, and many horrors in its name are being witnessed and increasingly perpetrated against Muslims in Burma, Muslims in China, Muslims in Palestine, Muslims in Yemen, and persons of all faiths in Syria and Iraq. Some of these abuses appear as ethnic tensions, or immigration troubles, or the general disinterest and inability of sovereign states to protect rights of those not recognized as entitled to citizenship. Many of these abuses are at the hands of Muslim nationalists making the despicable claim that they are acting under G'd's authority of 'jihad.' It is absolutely necessary for me to speak on this issue where Muslim attitudes and behaviors are in focus and the protection of so-called Muslim interests and identity are said to be the concern at stake but in actuality the objectives being pursued by Muslims are not viable or recognizable as Islamic interests.

Prophet Muhammed had no interest or stake in the ideologies of pursuit of world domination, other than to oppose them. His interest was the establishment of the human individual in the dignity of human community, as G'd intended for Adam and his mate in the Garden.

The international terrorist groups operating on every continent that claim to want to establish an Islamic State are nothing more than nationalist 'Crusaders' with Muslim names, and their wars against innocent populations have nothing to do with the Islamic concept of jihad.

Jihad is principled and legitimate struggle intended to serve G'd by freeing the innocent from abuse and forced restraint of their natural rights to self-determination as human beings. Jihad is not nationalism. Jihad is not militarism. Jihad is not an indiscriminate arming of civilians, and it is not law and order for the rule of police-states to intimidate un-armed civilians. Jihad is not revolution in the style of the socialists. Jihad is not rebellion in the style of the anarchists. Jihad's moral perfection cannot tolerate morally-ambiguous justifications for assaults on innocents, or state-sponsored murder, or extra-judicial pronouncements of guilt and executions, or any war-time excuse-making for collateral damage where innocent human beings are killed.

There is no legitimate jihad to oppose freedom, justice, and equality as an urge in the oppressed. The consciousness of those engaged in jihad is to govern their struggle by the rules of universal and ethical decency. Jihad is not the ends justify the means or the means justify the ends. If the means to a just end threaten to betray the integrity of the objective, then there is no jihad -there is only egregious sin. If the ends are worthy of G'd's approval for human dignity then the means must submit to and obey the end's moral authority.

Jihad is obedience to the highest moral and ethical principles approved by G'd for just service and struggle against evil and wrongdoing. Jihad is a struggle for justice that favors no worldly power or their systems -no matter if they claim it to be Islamic Shariah, above human entitlement to what G'd intended as a human spiritual, social, and material destiny for every human being on this earth by nature and birth. Jihad is not a Crusader-spirit seeking a national or imperial dominance or a method to impose the will of Muslims and their notion of faith on a population or an individual.

The jihad is to inform, and then to appeal to an informed conscience, and then to protect the innocence and rights of choice.

Jihad in the language and use of nationalists is false and illegitimate! Jihad cannot function as a nationalist tool, nor will it contort to satisfy the nationalist's need for a weapon against the innocent.

What has happened to the conscience and determinations of our Muslim leaders who have not made the objectives of jihad clear and exposed the deviations that have been wrongly associated with jihad? They shy from the discussion as if the word 'jihad' is an abominable evil. What is wrong with Muslim leaders, that with the evident rise of new nationalist sentiments in Europe and America, that they have not publicly called on the international following of Jesus Christ, to see, identify, and condemn this clear and present nationalist-Crusader-mentality and its reckless language of an artificial patriotism. Who in this world is better equipped to inform the political establishment and leadership of the dangers of nationalism, and the present conditions in the world that are favoring its revival than the educated followers of G'd's Messengers?

This is why the following of Imam W. Deen Mohammed are a sign to the innocent and the G'd-fearing.

Upon becoming the new leader of the Nation of Islam following -Supreme Minister as the title was given at that time, in February, 1975 -a community built upon the leadership of his father and obedience to his teacher, Mr. W. D. Fard, it was a deliberate act of faith and defining act of leadership when Wallace D. Mohammed re-designated that following *"The World Community of al-Islam in the West (WCIW)"*. By this one act in a series of guided decisions, his father's following became his people, taking the initial steps for turning them away from all vestiges of the regimented nationalism of the Nation of Islam image, to their natural Muslim identity and connections.

While Imam Mohammed understood that corrections in the teaching of Islamic faith were not confined to only the verbal declarations of faith, a close reading of his language over 33 years also proves that from the earliest moments he did not accept that his father's work should be so closely associated with the idea of 'black nationalism'. He insisted that his father was leader and builder of the "Temples of Islam", associating the Honorable Elijah Muhammad with the people as 'temple' in their Muslim religious identity, over the people as 'nation' in their American so-called Negro identity. He understood and interpreted his father's work within the context of the category of dignity G'd created for man that was denied the so-called Negro or black people of America to which they were entitled by nature.

He understood the Honorable Elijah Muhammad as obeying the language and strategies of his teacher, but that he used his own mind to identify the American so-called Negro as a people obstructed from their human entitlements and citizenship supports, and therefore especially entitled to be chosen by G'd and designated by Him as a "Nation" that would command the rights and respect of any people in a normal 'national' dignity. That teaching in the "Nation of Islam" that is commonly associated with 'black nationalism' did not comport with the Honorable Elijah Muhammad's emphasis, nor did it transfer to Imam W. Deen Mohammed's leadership or teaching.

Imam W. Deen Mohammed did not accept that identification of the need for post-slavery identity reconstruction and the dignity of social and economic establishments in the African-American people were an offspring or a dependent of nationalist ideology. He taught that these are natural inclinations and aspirations and are properties on demand in the nature of all human beings and human communities. He clearly identified and explained the Islamic teachings which enshrine the principle that the natural entitlements or rights of human beings are an inheritance promised to Adam and all of his descendants. He did not explain this as metaphor, but as a reality to be worked for, earned, and brought into a social and material reality as citizens in America.

G'd says in the Holy Qur'an, explicitly, that all of Adam's descendants have been given special favor and that they are all honored. Within this context Imam Mohammed explained how our identification as Americans is defined. He made clear that as Muslims we are not seeking an American national identity because we are in some way lacking language in Islam for our human identity. No! It is well known that American and U.S. Constitutional law did not always protect or value our humanity. And as evidenced by 'nationalist' trends in America right now, if there is not a strong patriotic community of Americans awake to protect the high and correct principle that all human life has been 'endowed by its Creator with certain unalienable rights', then a wave of artificial patriotism that favors one majority nationalist group in America will threaten the abolishment of those fundamental recognitions, just as they were historically and deliberately denied the African-American people.

As Muslim-Americans, Imam W. Deen Mohammed taught that the Holy Qur'an is sufficient as language for us to inform our human worth, with the U.S. Constitution as the foundation for a system of laws reflecting the American Founder's perception of Divine guarantees and governing a people and ensuring their common access to the rights and protections of citizenship.

He taught that the fundamental constitution of our life as G'd made it precedes all governments and all nations, just as the ideas characterizing 'democracy' preceded the thinking of America's Founders, and that our human identity is best clothed with awareness and love for G'd and all that He has created that is shared and cherished by all civilized people in society.

Imam Mohammed taught that we are Americans as this world requires and regulates entries and exits in its mutual and cooperative systems of citizen movement, and the movement of resources and ideas, and our own specific and unique struggle to overcome obstacles to realizing full citizenship. But, our interpretation of our American-ness does not accept a superiority over our human-ness; and our human-ness is defined and focused by our G'd-Designed Muslim nature; and the Islamic identity that forms us as a community of Muslim-Americans also energizes our citizenship and sense of patriotism. Our patriotism in America is not nationalist. It is a thoughtful loyalty to the ideas that comport with the way in which man is instructed by G'd to participate and contribute to the well-being of society.

While Imam W. Deen Mohammed dealt with the issue of identifying his people to observers, he was never satisfied that any organizational identity suited his people, their history, their purpose, and their worth. He settled that we are a "new people," and I have mentioned this and what it means many times over the last several months.

Imam Mohammed was well-acquainted with the opportunities an organizational identity offered to evil-doers to infiltrate its life and manifest themselves in the form of oppressive ideas and personalities affecting his people's thinking and directing them to other than a true Islamic destiny. He identified his following in our legitimate group aspirations and ethnic bonds, in our common circumstances and history, and our group needs for social and economic establishments. His teaching lives in his Muslim-American people.

We are an organic, living body -not diminished or limited by any national organizational label, but growing in our Islamic religious identity that shares blood relations, affection for country and countrymen, American citizenship ties and responsibilities, with permanent interests that are best described as ethical, humane, universal, and Islamic. **Our community is G'd's sign in the earth for the innocent and those that regard G'd.**

We invite those who see the evidence in America and the world, and perhaps feel threatened or manipulated by the de-constructive forces of nationalist ideas to take a close look at us and our message. And we pray that Allah guide you, protect you, and preserve you for the best human life in the country and home you choose for yourself.

8 Muhammed the Prophet is Nearest to Jesus the Christ

"In this world and the Hereafter, I am the nearest to Jesus the son of Maryam. The Prophets are paternal brothers. Their mothers are different but their Religion is One."

Muhammed the Prophet

As-Salaam Alaikum. That is Peace be on you. We greet our honorable audience. We thank Allah for this opportunity to speak to you. We thank Him, He that is the Lord of all the Systems of Knowledge, Highly Glorified and Praised is He.

Praise be to Allah. We seek His Aid. We ask His forgiveness. We rely upon Him. We put our trust in Him. We believe in Him. He is Highly Glorified and Praised. For Him is the Might and the Power. For Him is the Rule. For Him is the Creation and the Command. We witness that there is nothing to be joined with Him in His Rule and His Command. We witness that nothing is deserving of our worship except Him. He has created us with a nature to obey and an intellect to conclude the matter as to what we should give our obedience. We have been created with purpose, no matter what the disbelievers allege or attempt to prove.

The disbelievers want us to adopt their conclusions about human purpose. They want us to question G'd's Command in our nature, and to be suspicious of G'd's Authority. If we have the blessing of the purity of our nature working for us, then we know instinctively -by nature, that we should not obey that which takes us out of good, human form.

Even the new baby will express his or her discomfort with that which doesn't suit their nature. Babies have no tolerance for filth. This is a sign in our nature in its pristine state of its inherent desire for purity and excellence. Our pure, human nature that G'd created draws us to an excellence.

I am speaking of excellence as a property in our nature. It is an excellence that G'd created in us and that works for us. He created that excellence for us, and He missioned all of the Prophets and Messengers to reach for that excellence. And they are all types in the human mission and exercise toward realizing the highest human excellence -the highest human performance. Allah intended that we would eventually see that our nature accommodates increasing degrees of excellence. And Muhammed is the best of creation, the best in the demonstration of human excellence.

Muhammed, the son of Abdullah of the Arab lineage, upon him the choicest blessings and salute, and the peace. Muhammed stands upon the natural pattern which seeks for Guidance so as to arrive at the intended human conclusion for an honorable existence in this world, a beautiful human world. Muhammed, if we will see him properly, is a sign of the beautiful human world of human life in society. And this is the picture of the Home of the G'd-fearing, the blessed 'dar ul-mutaqeen'.

We witness that Muhammed is G'd's Messenger, and that he has no divine nature. He is G'd's servant, His slave. He is the picture of human perfection that G'd intended for human nature. That perfection is human perfection, not divine perfection.

Muhammed's life says that G'd intended that human life have its perfect destiny and conclusion without claiming to be anything more than a pure human being relying on nature, and then relying on G'd's Guidance in His Plan.

Someone may read the title of this address and think that I am speaking about inter-faith work or weekly inter-faith meetings. That would be an incorrect conclusion. I am not addressing a need for Muslim-Christian-Jewish dialogue or unity. We have much of that today, but it is not my focus here. Please do not misunderstand what I am saying. I can hear one of you who dislike that Allah is helping me saying, "See, did you hear that? He is saying that we don't need to have inter-faith efforts. That's not the Imam..."

That is far away from what I am saying. It is an important concern and certainly we should always respond to opportunities and invitations for dialogue and productive, meaningful engagement between the peoples of faith in G'd. We invite exchange with the G'd-fearing people and our disposition with them is always openness to these opportunities. We cannot have the beautiful world that the people of faith are promised and led to see in the Revelation without us maintaining that basic interest and openness and readiness to invite one another for discussion, mutual education, and general problem-solving.

But I am referring to something else here. The inter-faith movements and activities cannot be successful in the call for an increased awareness to universal human interests and concerns if they are not perceiving a conclusion or destiny for man, that is, in man's collective soul, in this world.

I am speaking of the conclusions for human life that we recognize by nature - a sense in our moral or emotional nature, before our rational nature has evolved and been educated to produce language to describe it. This sense dawns in the expressions of all people. Rational sciences give us language to characterize it, but it is first conceived in the emotional nature, in the seat of moral intelligence -the heart.

Anthropology is a science studying what is common to man in his developmental and directional nature. So is the science of psychology, though it is focused more specifically on the mind. But the mind -the thinking, is a product of what is fundamental to the nature as the nature responds to the natural environment and also what man has done in the environment both good and bad. These are sciences of the collective human soul. The desire in us to understand ourselves in a fundamental way is a function in man's universal soul -the forces that are common to human nature and transcend ethnicity and race and national origin.

In fact, when you recognize the reality of man's universal soul you realize that these other designations are fleeting and more illusion than actual. Man focused or characterized in a racial or ethnic reality is not man in his original, fundamental nature. Nowhere in the Holy Qur'an teaching is man addressed in a racial category. Man's distinctions are addressed, but in the context of correctly characterizing his origin and destiny as an entity only capable of realizing his highest potential when he adheres to the call of his Lord Who is calling to him in his collective, universal nature.

We cannot see Adam in a racial picture. He is the original human type as male and female from which mankind develops. The moral and rational sciences, we may say anthropology and psychology and the language and interests of these sciences, develop from Adam as the original soul. The early thinkers in the history of al-Islam, the early people of science and reason, and their reach in the world with Muslim identity were not motivated by any dominance in the earth. They were not after a military order and rule, or empire building in the earth. They recited and reflected on the words in the Holy Qur'an that Allah says He has subjected what is in the skies and the earth, what comes from the sun and the moon, what is in the night and the day, what lives in the sea and can be drawn from the power of the rivers, what is in the mountains, what is in the meaning of colors, and what knowledge can be extracted from all of Creation for man's use and benefit.

They understood from all of that that their important responsibility was to uncover what the Merciful Benefactor deposited there for them to benefit from, and they understood the nature of their stewardship under G'd's authority in the earth to serve all human beings for the conclusions of human life. They understood that in all of Creation there are Signs holding knowledge, and there are also signs of what is inside man's soul and inside his nature as properties to form patterns of logic leading to a conclusion.

They understood G'd's ultimate expectation of man as a discipline in his nature to reach for a fulfillment, to reach for a destiny. They saw this in the Holy Qur'an and the Prophet's teaching. And because of this teaching, they more fully understood G'd's Love and Care for man. This led to their understanding that G'd intended that they feel authorized in their moral and intellectual nature to name these forces, these sciences, that direct man to his purpose. And they named them *'ilm ul-insaan* -science of man or what we call anthropology, and *'ilm un-nafs* -science of the self or what we call psychology.

They understood that when we are looking at Adam we should see or perceive the universal, common, dynamic human soul, and that that soul has a destiny, a conclusion, a plan that G'd intended for it. That soul has a potential that is both light and darkness. If you are not managing the potential in that soul for its intended purpose that potential will show itself as darkness, and it will oppress and burden man's life. And if you are managing its potential as G'd intends it then it is a beacon of light that frees man's life for progress and development.

They came to understand that the properties of man's soul are to be discovered, articulated, and acted upon through bonds in cooperation between individuals and groups who are correctly educated and positioned in their moral nature to see and perceive man in his destiny on earth.

So, therefore inter-faith efforts that only focus on reading the Word of G'd to each other or sharing our intellectual perspectives on Scripture, or theorizing on abstract spiritual or theological themes, etc. will not be effective by themselves. We should be concerned to not allow the importance of our inter-faith efforts and activities to be limited. They are important opportunities for cultivating understanding and cooperation.

Muslims who participate in inter-faith intellectual exchanges with no objective other than the intellectual exchange actually damage the image of Islam, misappropriate Islamic teaching, and misinterpret Islamic emphasis.

Islamic teaching first focuses the heart in its intelligent properties that are amenable and pliable -soft like clay ready to be formed, then it quickens and fixes and guides the intellect to solidify as leadership in preparation, then principled action toward fulfillment of the support and service needed by real-life human beings in human communities. Inter-faith dialogues that attract participants who only desire to impress each other with their eloquence, hurt all of us.

Too much of inter-faith discussion has been weakened because the ability to pinpoint what is important to comprehend for the conclusion for human life is not spoken of in its proper frame. Jewish moral teaching, Christian moral teaching, Islamic moral teachings are essential for influencing human life toward truth and to embrace just ends.

This is confirmed in the Holy Qur'an. Our inter-faith works must be strengthened, and aimed at gaining traction against schemes of mischief in the world. As Muslims we have no teaching or mission to unmask evil. But we are asked to resist and repel evil in the interest of protecting the sanctity of human life, human existence, and human purpose. We are not asked to concentrate on revealing the identity of the Deceiver. He has many identities, and he uses all of them simultaneously to confuse man about the worth of man's nature, and to redirect man's nature for conclusions that confuse, or weaken, or destroy human lives. His schemes poison human thinking and human society.

Our nature has been empowered by G'd to turn from the influence of the schemes of the Deceiver and to fight his schemes. The Deceiver is too skilled and experienced in his multiple identities that attack man's nature to subject himself to sit still and be identified in one picture. We know that his form is in at least three realities -small, medium, and large, and that with the principle in man's nature that is expressed in seven elevations or urges of moral intelligence, G'd has empowered man to free himself and his society of Satan's call.

This is preserved in our Islamic teaching and ritual. This public address is not for explanations of all of these matters. Soon we will have an opportunity to address these matters in the classes and addresses we are planning that will continue in the manner that Imam W. Deen Mohammed taught his people.

I believe it is time, and it is appropriate in this context to digress a bit and speak directly to what I am doing and a few things about my circumstances. There are many people throughout this land who appreciate me, and respect what I am doing and are letting me know of their love and strong, committed support.

I fully intend to fulfill what they recognize as Imam W. Deen Mohammed's expectations of me in serving the leadership need in the life of his people through the proper use and understanding of his language of Islamic teaching. And so, we are responding to invitations and planning public meetings -public addresses, right now, all over this nation. We have invitations that we cannot answer now but that we will answer to places outside of this country. And we are planning our Ramadan gatherings and cultural gatherings and Islamic classes right now in the interest of addressing and serving his expectations for our community.

This is not my plan. It is Allah's Plan for our people that this be done in order that our purposes and interests as a Muslim-African-American people, a Muslim-Bilalian people, are represented and focused properly. I know that there are many who cannot and will not see it. They are blinded and cursed. But the fair-minded people sense that nothing of what I have been doing would be possible except that Allah has directed it, protected it, and protected me.

Our people should not appear confused about my interests or intentions. We should not want confusion. We should not allow confusion. The simple fact of the matter is that Allah has helped me directly for this work in this time, and He has directly protected me. He has protected my heart and my mind for this purpose. He has preserved my sincerity and innocence for this purpose. He has sent me help for this purpose. It is Allah's Plan that my Islamic moral sensitivities -my humanity, has been guarded and nourished in such a way that I am able to speak with the clarity and certainty that I do in spite of the fact that I am a prisoner of the United States Federal Government, and in spite of those who wish to see me silenced or dead.

It is His Plan that no criticizer can dilute my message or weaken the reach and effectiveness of my words though I have no way to avoid the limitations and constraints of a prisoner's life.

For every one of the ignorant or misinformed persons who criticize me or for those who are actively plotting to stop me, there are three or four strong supporters making themselves known publicly that they stand with me without fear or reservation. There are also the growing numbers of people who have never met me and who have no will to dispute with truth and clarity when they are exposed to it. These people -many of them younger people in their 20's and 30's, have no fear to acknowledge and embrace that truth and point to and align themselves with the first leader they have had any real confidence in since Imam W. Deen Mohammed.

It is Allah's Plan that my language is an authentic, proven, and irrefutable reflection of the knowledge and language of Imam W. Deen Mohammed. It is Allah's Plan that my use of his knowledge and language is so evidently distinguished from others, making absolutely clear what is correct and incorrect understanding. My sensitivity for him is of such maturity that I do not have to struggle to find him. I am living and thinking and reasoning in his guided language and tradition. This would not be possible except that Allah has accepted my intentions as pure. It is His Plan that my use of Imam Mohammed's language is pristine, not in any way corrupted, artificial, contrived, pretended, guessed at, or illegitimate; and not misrepresenting, misunderstanding, or misusing that language, or diminishing what he -the guided Imam of al-Islam, *al-Mujeddid-ul-Islam,* intended as its precise and exact understanding and usage.

It is Allah's Plan that a group of informed, experienced, and confident men and women of faith and determination, who have proven immovable in their convictions and impermeable by forces of fear and negativity, have formed as a firm, cemented structure supporting me. They recognize me as the leader that Imam W. Deen Mohammed identified for his people after him, and they are readying themselves for my release from prison and preparing with me to face what is ahead. It is Allah that has filled them with a spirit of assurance that we are on a straight and correct path -the path designated and approved by Him; and they are without any doubts in their conviction that I am the one Imam Mohammed spoke of that Allah would show us that we should support.

It is Allah's Plan that these men and women of faith cannot be influenced to withdraw their support despite the criticisms of many criticizers and veiled threats that they will be singled out and ostracized. Without fear or hesitation restricting them they gain in strength each time they hear or read my words, and they feel obligated because of their faith in Allah to share, promote, and defend me and my words.

I am thankful to Allah and I am humbled before Him, Highly Glorified and Praised is He, the Lord of all the Systems of Knowledge, the Lord of the Throne of Authority. I bow and prostrate before Him in His Majesty, and His Ownership of the universal human soul, and I pledge and devote my intent and works to His Approval, and I turn to Him in my conscious mind and submit to Him my subconscious and unconscious mind.

I ask that He Guide us, and Save us from the harm of our own errors and shortcomings, and to Protect us from any trap that the Enemy may set for us. I seek His Help and I rely on Him. And I ask Him to Grant His Mercy to the one who lived with us and taught us and led us to faith and identity and language and purpose -Imam W. Deen Mohammed.

Continuing now to address our topic, it has been said by some in the political and religious leadership of the Muslim world that America is the Satan. Satan is in America, there is no doubt. But he is also among those in the Muslim world who say this about America too. Satan's form in America may be different from his form in those places and among those persons, but if their leadership who speak of America in this way are not conscious and do not care how that language may affect Muslims in America and their good plans to contribute to a good future and beautiful condition for human beings in America, then it is plain to see how the Satan has manifest among them too.

That is not to say that what they are pointing to in America is not the Satan. We are not excusing America where it accommodates the Satan. The idea that encourages man to express his freedom in ways that corrupt his human picture and deform his human life far from the picture and form G'd intended when He created man is the influence of Satan.

I can think of ten or more very serious, destructive, and obvious ways in which Satan's influence is real and active among the common people and among the leaders in America. So, we are not excusing America. No, indeed! But we cannot conclude that America is Satan.

The good and decent people who have never strayed from G'd's purpose for man who are Americans prove that statement to be untrue. And we would never think of ourselves as the Satan or under the authority of Satan or his followers. That is a sickening, repulsive notion.

But we are tested by the reality of his influence, and we fight his schemes in America, and we identify those schemes in how they affect and disrupt or confuse human life from realizing its G'd-given purpose. This is why we are not asked to identify Satan or unmask him. G'd has identified him for us, if we will pay attention. As soon as you think you know the true identity of the Satan he shifts to some other picture, and in many cases the picture you thought he was will be looking back at you as a guiltless saint. And if you attack that picture you will become the guilty party. G'd does not leave us vulnerable in this way.

As the Holy Qur'an says, G'd asks us to fight his schemes. His schemes are in any idea or trend or philosophy or influence which attempt to weaken our perception and understanding of true human purpose as planned by G'd or directs us to a behavior or a pattern of thinking that undresses our created and natural human dignity.

The great communities and peoples of faith are assigned the responsibility of engagement to defeat the Satan's schemes. We encourage our publics of faith to commit themselves and to require of each other sincere commitments addressing real-life needs with clear moral reasoning. Our common humanity places common demands on all of us who are conscious. No matter what community of faith we belong to, or what nation we live in or are citizens of, or in what way we characterize ourselves racially or culturally, our human destiny in the earth is all the same as one universal human community. The moral and intellectual urges in man's soul, in his consciousness as a human type, bring him and his society to this awareness. His social urges bring him to this conclusion.

Even the material glitter which embellishes the world and inspires in man material interests and pursuits that may lead some to pursue a dominance and command in the earth and its resources, are nothing but a test for man in his recognition of a common and universal destiny. There are no systems in today's world that do not touch all human life, or cannot be seen or detected or sensed by human life no matter in what remote places we may be living.

One small nation can affect the global reality of man. One seemingly insignificant act can stir global economic markets and shake and convulse man's sense of comfort. Today, and as pointed to by the great thinkers and leaders, man's life is a single expression in one, global, universal reality.

Allah says in the Holy Qur'an and no teacher of Islam in the modern age said it more clearly and directly than Imam W. Deen Mohammed that G'd has constructed our nature in such a way that we are bonded in our universality as a single soul. We are created from an original, single soul and our destiny is to be raised as a single, universal soul.

It is reported that Muhammed the Prophet said: *"Both in this world and the Hereafter I am the nearest of all the people to Jesus, the son of Mary. The Prophets are paternal brothers; their mothers are different, but their religion is one."*

Our Prophet is identifying and teaching about the principle in the human nature that it makes no discernible difference from what social reality or womb you are birthed, the destiny of man's life is in one collective global and universal conclusion, and Jesus with Muhammed is a sign of that conclusion. It has its temporal or material component and its spiritual component. Business people planning their business future and success cannot avoid respecting that mankind is one on the earth. Their businesses risk failure if they are not studying and appealing to man in his universal destiny.

Governments cannot avoid interactions with each other, even if they act as if they are enemies. Government leaders generally understand that ultimately the global community will rise as one community of man against any single rogue government which demonstrates or threatens a refusal to honor man's universal destiny and put man as a global community at risk. Does this mean that man will not have conflicts? No.

This does not mean that the Satan will not do all in his ability to confuse the matter. But the Prophet's teaching is clear. Even with issues of contention between nations which burden and plague man's world, the universal human soul demands progress toward the destiny G'd fashioned for it. In spite of our different mothers -according to the Prophet's teaching, what Jesus represents in the world and the Hereafter will reconcile itself to Muhammed's purpose in the world and the Hereafter -in the material earth as a conclusion and in the soul as a destiny. It is given in the Bible -this is not the Holy Qur'an teaching specifically, that Jesus the Christ was transformed from a flesh body to a configuration of light.

As Muslims we have authorization to look at the Bible. Don't let anyone make you think that we are somehow outside of our Islamic life if we look at the Bible. We are looking at it in its purity and not in what has been introduced into it of corruption. We are protected from corruption by the Holy Qur'an. If we have the

Holy Qur'an as the guide with which we look at the Bible we are safe for the purpose that Allah wants for us.

If we are looking at the Prophets through Muhammed the Prophet's teaching we are understanding correctly. The Prophet, the highest salute and choicest blessings be on him, instructed his following that there is no clarity for understanding of what preceded the Holy Qur'an except that the Holy Qur'an and his teaching lead the way to that understanding.

Once, Umar bin al-Khattab -the great companion of the Prophet and second successive leader after the Prophet -may Allah be pleased with him, brought a reading from the Jewish scripture to the Prophet. The Prophet made clear to him that if Moses were present, he would be in Muhammed's following. So, there is no reality for the conclusion of the moral urge for freedom or leadership or establishments in the world except with Muhammed and what he has authorized.

So, here we have Jesus as a configuration of light, and the light is of no use to man for him to just admire it or look at it. In fact, if you look at it directly it will punish you. True light will punish your eyes if you look directly at it. The benefit of the light is not in looking at it directly; the benefit is in what it 'illuminates' for us to see. And joined with Jesus as light in this Bible presentation are Moses and Elijah, peace be on the Prophets.

This is the picture as it is given in this story in the Bible: Jesus transformed from a flesh body to a light configuration and the Prophets Moses and Elijah in the same reference. Three movements in the social and moral urges of man that conclude in light. Moses -a social urge in the world for leadership, freedom and just establishments, and Elijah -a moral urge to destroy confusion in correct perceptions of G'd's Will and Authority in man's universal soul and destiny, and Jesus as the light of Guidance.

Where do we see, or where is the light to see these three urges in man in one frame of reference? It is in the Holy Qur'an. This

Bible story is pointing to the conclusion for man's life in the Book that was revealed to Muhammed and establishes Muhammed as the Seal of the Prophets.

Muhammed the Prophet's demonstration of human perfection, or excellence, is the enhancement and filter for the light - the light that when it is shown through a prism separating its productive properties of benefit in man's world, shows itself as guidance to identify the moral demand in our nature for freedom and leadership toward a productive, beautiful, honorable, universal existence. But in order to bring out that beautiful existence our nature must also be turned on to recognize, seek, and obey G'd's Will and Authority and His Plan for man's destiny. We must search out and defeat the falsehoods, the schemes, and subject them to G'd's judgment.

This is light for mankind, but we will not see where the light is pointing if we do not have Imam W. Deen Mohammed's influence in our lives and the guided tradition that came with him that is the proof of Allah's favor on us. That struggle in the flesh, material reality to make sense of its material purpose will push you and bring you to a light that has spiritual properties, and answers, or provides clarification, as to what are proper perceptions for your reality in the material existence.

The Deceiver will point us to some reasoning that will blind us and we will perceive the light as darkness. That is what blindness is. Blindness is darkness. And to the deceived ones -the blind and the blinded, they see the darkness as light. And they use the darkness as if it is light. This is one of the signs of the Last Days. This is the time we live in -the time of the conclusion. Man is brought to the conclusion by a struggle for correct perception in his moral and intellectual nature. You are designed to prevail in this struggle, but it is an uphill climb, a steep path. The Prophet said that in the Last Days the Deceiver will offer water and it will be fire.

So, our conclusion as a human community is with the Light in Muhammed's use, in Muhammed's demonstration. I know some who read this or hear this will not appreciate its importance or understand it properly. We are speaking in a language that you will have to allow yourself patience to become re-acquainted with. Most of you who read or hear this have been deliberately taken away from this understanding by witch-doctors so as to make use of your life for purposes other than what you are entitled. They have preyed on your innocence. If you choose language of understanding for Islamic teaching and Islamic understanding, especially as regards descriptions of the destiny all mankind has been created for, that does not respect your dignity and invites you to a perception of your Muslim identity where you must enslave yourself to courses of study and instructors where the end result is that you find yourself in conflict with every system, every institution, and every human being around you, then you have been given fire instead of water.

It is Prophet Muhammed who has been given the light as guidance for mankind to bring man to a proper and conclusive demonstration of the just order in the world. This just order is not for the private individual soul only. Man cannot have the just order in only his recognition of peace in the soul. He will see it or perceive it in the soul, but the Light exists in the material world and it is a material reality. We are flesh bodies in this world, so the just establishments must be spoken of, demonstrated, and experienced in our material form. In other words, all peoples on this earth are entitled to a dignified existence, a respected existence in society in this world.

Our spiritual orientations, if they are authentic, must awaken in us the obligation to bring comforts to human life in this world. We must be peace-makers and peace-guarantors. We must be breakers of slavery and slave systems with our language, if not with our works. Muslims who make war on innocence, will have a severe punishment, if not in this world, then the next. Christians who make war on the innocent will have a severe punishment, if not in this world, then the next. Jews who make war on the innocent will have a severe punishment, if not in this world, then the next. There is no hiding behind a righteous label and behaving or promoting a thinking that is unworthy of that label in the time of the Light and Muhammed together. Muhammed comes with the Light, but there is also the conclusion for its establishment.

The conclusion is in just establishments -the time where human life and all of its systems of knowledge and discovery must conform to the principle of the Light and Muhammed, or else they will be shown as impostors for man's good. All oppressors and liars will be exposed.

For the Muslims, you cannot claim that your society is under the authority of Islam without the test of that. It will be shown if that is true or false. You will be exposed. The knowledge which uphold your societies will be exposed for their inadequacies. It will be tested and exposed for its truth or falsehood. Only the Light with Muhammed will survive. What is essential as urges in the moral nature shown in Jesus as a light configuration with Moses and Elijah as witnesses pointing to Muhammed is the fulfillment of man's purpose. This is the destiny. This is the conclusion for the universal human soul. If you cheat Imam W. Deen Mohammed's knowledge, language, and leadership you will be exposed.

The notion of Jesus as Christ and Prophet Muhammed together in the world summons the just and good forces, the universal ethical army, to its mission. It is the call to all wombs of man -all nations, all races, all heavenly religions to reach for its highest and most clear ethical vision. It is not the end of good, it is the destiny for the good. It is the last curtain for racism, sexism, nationalism, the finish for the rule of the corrupt. By Light -proper education and focus that respects and loves and cares for human life, which calls together the urges for freedom and dignity and makes just war on lies and corruption in the highest standards of human expression and excellence, the conclusion for the soul is made clear for all to embrace and share in it.

Some of you who read or hear this may say it is a dream. Maybe, but it is the dream of the awakened people. And Joseph had an awakening that was a dream and he was given a light with which to interpret the material reality for its conclusions. He gave the society language and perspectives to save itself in a just order. And the society acknowledged Joseph as the concluding intellect; a sign of the intellect that saw the destiny and how to get there. And we cannot know this except that it is given in the Revelation given to Muhammed.

9   A New People

"And We wished to bestow a special help on those who were oppressed in the land, to make them leaders and contributors, and qualify them to be heirs, to establish for them a lasting place in the land."

Holy Qur'an 28:5-6

As-Salaam Alaikum. That is, peace be upon you. This is our traditional Islamic greeting spoken by all Muslims wherever we are in the world. And these are also signature words identifying a special group in the history of this country. These words identify a new mind and cultural influence, a new dignity, a new pride, and a new people in America. It didn't come from immigrants. Immigrant Muslims didn't appear here in great numbers until the 1960's and by that time the Honorable Elijah Muhammad and his following had been using this greeting with each other for 30 years. We say these words imperceptibly now, they are such a normal characteristic in our religious and cultural habits as Muslims. But they have very significant meaning for our religious life. With this greeting we are saluting G'd's purpose for each one of us, and we are asking G'd to preserve us for that purpose in each other and for each other.

These words, if we obey them in what they allude to, guarantee and secure a righteous existence, a peaceful existence; a peace-loving, G'd-centered society. We do not believe as Muslims that we come out of G'd. But we do believe that we have something from G'd. That He has given us something of Him in His attributes. G'd acquaints us with the power of peace and acknowledgment of Him over human society. These greetings make our concentration on peace an intimate matter. It is our peace to have for our individual lives, for our family lives, for our lives in society. See how wonderful our history is and what powerful presence our Muslim history has for America when we see these things in the correct way? When the first teachers in the Temple of Islam introduced these words, do you not see that they were greeting America: "As-Salaam Alaikum," for the first time?

Praise be to Allah. He is the Lord and Cherisher. We are introduced to Him firstly as our Lord. In Islamic teaching we do not know Allah as G'd before we know Him as Lord. He introduces Himself to Muhammed in the words of the Holy Qur'an as "the Lord Who Creates." In the Islamic meaning Lord says a Caring, Loving, Nurturing Presence that brings us along step-by-step to the destiny He fashioned for us.

He brings us from the first environment of care -the family, and evolves us upon education and to progress. And this is what this world took from us. It took this primary environment from us. It destroyed the social structures that our Lord created for all humanity to develop from. It took from us that natural system which Allah made to form people into a social reality -tribes and nations. The family of those enslaved in America's system of slavery was totally destroyed. But the world could not do that without G'd's permission. And so, we have been created again as a people in this way in America for some great, important purpose.

I intend to identify this meaning for our life in this address. But it would not be possible without the knowledge and language of Imam W. Deen Mohammed. These sensitivities cannot be expressed properly without him.

G'd permitted our condition and our circumstances as a people for language to form in us in order to speak the words that characterize man as G'd intends. A language of conscience spoken not in Arabic or English or any other of these languages; it is the purest of Islamic language spoken to a modern, international world lost to man's true purpose. His language is the language of knowledge of a new human community created by G'd to teach what human life has been created for.

We witness that nothing is to be worshipped except Allah, the Lord-Creator. And we witness that Muhammed is His Messenger. This testimony or 'shahadatain' as it is called is a language of transformation. It is to witness to a fundamental, inescapable truth that human life and progress are not possible without acknowledgment of G'd, and what He revealed for man to know about himself, his environment, and his creation to benefit from his human spiritual nature and the material environment. This truth transforms the human life from less to more, from good to better, from progressive to the highest performance in human excellence.

This understanding He revealed in the words of the Perfect and Clear Book, the Book with no defects, the Holy Qur'an. And He revealed the Holy Qur'an to Muhammed, His Messenger. We pray the choicest favor and blessings on him. He is the most excellent of human beings and the leader for human society and the example for that life in perfect demonstration, if we understand him.

And all language and knowledge for establishing the order of Peace and Mercy in man's world comes from him and his model life of human excellence and its teaching. We, his community are witnesses to him. If we fail in establishing the correct picture of human society it is because we are disobeying or falling short of his example.

We say that those descended from slaves and brought to an awakening of their human life destiny and purpose in the teachings of Islam in the continuity of community that began with Mr. W. D. Fard and his Lost-Found Nation of Islam, their conscious descendants, and all those identifying in its language environment of faith and direction, are a new people on the earth. To say that a new people inhabit the earth is a spiritual language and description because it first speaks to spiritual needs and sensitivities. It is spiritual truth, but it has deep significance and relevance in all aspects and expressions of human life.

Mr. W. D. Fard, the first teacher of the Nation of Islam idea, and his language could be and was confusing to the untrained and unauthorized observer. However, one aspect of his often confounding logic was clear, undeniable, and indisputable: To identify the slave-name, that is, the names forced upon enslaved Africans in America to identify them as the chattel property of slave traders and owners, as illegitimate, rejecting and marking that illegitimacy with an 'X', Mr. Fard was emphasizing and verifying that this people did not belong to the heritage of the plantation brand they had been forced to carry and produce for, nor could they or should they claim any entitlements or social benefits from identifying with it.

He wanted them to reject it, reject its very nature and foundations, and separate from its influence and authority in their lives. He taught them through his primary minister and obedient creation -the Honorable Elijah Muhammad, that their identity was 'X' and their worth as humans was 'X' -an unknown, unvalued property. They were neither African -because their Africanness had been ripped from them; nor American -because their American-ness had been denied them.

The names forced upon the slaves were brands on the faces of the enslaved, not to be confused or associated as any extended or dignified human, socio-cultural tradition. 'Sally' and 'Buck' So-and So -the 'typical' black slave mistress and field slave, were not the natural or legal mate of the slave master nor his legitimate employee; nor were the names given them a reflection of the heritage of their human selves. I am not speaking of the exceptions. I am identifying the general picture and intent of the slave world. Those names were intended as permanent brands upon those who had been reduced by slavery to an animal-level property, marked and trained to respond as an animal to its owner's call. The identity given the slaves by the slave-masters were not intended by the slave master to be reflective of any true human reality. It was solely to label them in their chattel slave reality. It was not meant to serve them as human beings in the manner that names serve human community identity in social progress.

This was the logic of the Temple of Islam. And in this new language-world, the language-world of American-style oppression as confronted by the natural urge to see G'd's will by way of Temple of Islam perceptions and determinations, the language of Imam W. Deen Mohammed's knowledge began to form.

Muhammed the Prophet, the prayers and the peace be on him, forbade the branding of the faces of animals designated for labor. He asked for Allah's curse on a woman who confined a cat in her home with no provisions, and prevented that cat from seeking its own cat-dignity with free access to the natural world.

Islam requires progressive and substantial movement against any form of oppression -physical, mental, spiritual, psychological, or material. A society satisfied with or insisting that it retain any form of slavery for a human being is not and can never be a true Islamic society. Such a society is not under an Islamic authority no matter what it may claim. I know someone who reads this or hears this address will say, "Islam authorizes slavery." You have been misinformed. Or, you may be a devil. I know that those who want us to abandon faith and the way of faith in G'd say this. But let me inform you: Islam wants dignity for human labor, and it requires the cultivation of moral sensitivities to abolish the notion that a created human soul inspired and guided by G'd's Word, is created to be anything less than G'd's slave-servant. Islam teaches that it is beneath human dignity to barter for any identity other than human identity and all of its respected properties. It is the honor conferred on Adam and all of his descendants. Family names record for us that a generation of peoples belongs to the generation of that same people before them. Essential traditions of social life are formed from celebrating these names.

Traditions marking new milestones of progress are in the group identity as family names. In this way even the oppressed retain a semblance of their lives even under brutal abuses. This is true of the Native Americans, South Africans, and more recently the Rohingya Muslims of Myanmar (or Burma) and Uyghur Muslims of China. They have been and are oppressed peoples, but while their struggles to throw oppression off of them may constitute for them a new reality, they are not new human communities. They remain a distinct people in spite of displacement and abuse.

Many peoples have been renewed by fresh ideas, and they have been enabled to remake themselves socially, and rise in degrees of human excellence. So, to say there is such a thing as a new people is not necessarily new language. But, the standing of the people of Imam W. Deen Mohammed is language of a new human creation spoken for the first time in legitimacy since the time of Muhammed the Prophet.

Muhammed was the new life for humanity in his person, in his leadership, in his nature, in his intellect, and in his universal mission to humanity. He is the example and model of human excellence. The Arabs were remade as a human community because of the Prophet's influence and teaching in their lives, but they were not a new human creation. The Arabic language was perfected by the Holy Qur'an, its communicative properties concentrated and expanded by the miracle of Divine Guidance, and the Arabs retained their Arabic tongue but with a new and profound elevation of knowledge supported by the Revelation. Their influence has been felt on all continents and by their efforts Islam has been introduced and been the factor in transforming many human lives and societies.

Africa is an example. The Africans, who had built and ruled advanced civilizations, witnessed the momentous changes in the character of the Arab's moral and intellectual reach. This change in the Arab moral conscience impressed the African and ultimately was a key in re-fashioning them as new African peoples in Islam. As functioning Muslim societies, they reached new heights of knowledge and rose to even greater heights of moral awareness and material progress, re-categorizing their new achievements in the sciences as favor on them from G'd, and dismissing old notions of themselves as gods.

But even they, though reformed and renewed as great African peoples, were not a new human creation. I could give more examples of ancient and even more modern peoples who by some important social or political forces, or potent trends of change were transformed in some powerful way, and became a new and improved version of themselves as witnessed by other peoples on the universal, human stage.

After World War II, because of spiritual, social, and financial pressures coming from the Christian West and a reordering of the world's power bases, Germany was a defeated people. It may well have been coerced, but it became a new people, but not a new human creation. In the last half century, the people of Cuba, in a few short years of revolution by way of the sciences of political messaging and social dynamics, became a new people speaking a new, infectious language into the ears of oppressed minorities worldwide. Their political language influenced many throughout the world, romancing even African-American intellects, but, they as a new Cuban people, were not a new human creation.

All of these groups I have mentioned retained their human life traditions. In many ways their human social identity was improved or refreshed or renewed. But, unlike the group formed from the womb of African-American struggle, none of them are a new human creation.

I am saying with the support of the history of social movements in the world, and even the history of Islamic achievements and progress, that this world has not known a people like us before.

I know that there will be African-Americans who cannot permit themselves to see an existence separated from the authority of the white race's analysis of human history, and so they will reject what I am suggesting in this address. They will lament the white world's abuses and concede the historical record of slavery and oppression, but they cannot see themselves as anything other than the creation of the white world. And so, they remain locked into a psychological slave identity where their only salvation is the white world's misrepresentation of their worth, an inferior being programmed and destined to serve anything and everything but its own good interests.

This psychological slave does not beg G'd for Guidance to free himself so as to stand in the dignity of his own human nature and excellence. He has been trained to beg the man-god image branded in his psyche for any modicum of presence in his society, even if that be an animal-level people cloaked in a gilded straightjacket of artificial, vulnerable social establishments.

It is not the animal that I am criticizing because that animal is obeying the nature G'd created for him. No, I am identifying that Negro creation of the white world who has evidence all around him of the autonomous human-community dignity G'd created him for, but undresses and refuses that dignity and chooses to be only a cheap reflection of someone else's self.

We are a people destined to be ourselves, and no matter what level of eloquence we acquire to appeal to all others to want us, we will be rejected. We will be rejected by this world unless and until we embrace our true destiny. It is given in the Reading preceding the Holy Qur'an that the "the stone that the builders rejected becomes the cornerstone of the House of G'd."

This is not talking about a black people in America, as such, but it is identifying a new people in human creation who are the harvest from the black people of America. This is a people who would be denied access to the potent nature G'd created to serve humanity. The nature was poisoned for their use, and therefore could not be used effectively by them or for them. The productive properties of their nature were killed, dead to its true purpose, so the builders of this world cast it aside as a worthless stone. This is a people cast aside from the proper association with their created dignity, separated from that which is required to build a human community. And then when mankind in totality became lost to the human design because of the societal influences that forced the black people enslaved in America out of their nature, G'd restored that nature to them in a new language of understanding, and they became the symbolic-stone by which the new order of humanity aligned itself. And they would rise upon the power of the meaning of that symbolic-stone and House as Guidance, in the tradition and teachings of Muhammed the Prophet, and they would witness for themselves and explain in their new language the great elevations and destiny for man as established in the symbolic structure and order in the heavens. We are speaking of that stone which was placed in its proper designation by Muhammed's hands.

That stone that was kissed by Muhammed. That stone and House that all representatives in the human family cherish and salute. That stone and House that preserves in symbol man's precious original pattern and purpose. And G'd says in the Holy Qur'an that the House was placed there, full of Blessings and Guidance for mankind, in an uncultivated valley.

America has said it accepts everyone in the equality of their humanity, but our experiences and recently others' experiences are saying something other than this. We are addressing this, and we see that there is something terribly wrong with this America, but I am not saying that we shouldn't love America and contribute to it. The reality I am pointing to is not political in nature. It is spiritual in nature with political implications. It is spiritual in nature with social implications. It is spiritual in nature with material implications. We should cherish our citizenship and look out for the best interests of our Muslim-American and American identity, and defend our place in America as native Americans, and defend America as a democratic idea in society.

But what I am referring to is in the spirit of a people seeing themselves as qualified and entitled to negotiate our citizenship contract with America just like other citizens. We have been formed as a people in America's spiritual environment even as America denied us the rights to a citizenship contract. The spiritual reality of America's environment in forming us as a people is registered by all who encounter us. It is because it extends beyond the physical. Its abuses register in the psyche of the people and they wear and display it in their knowledge and behavior.

It doesn't even matter what religion your mouth professes, if your heart is dead to your true nature you will be second-class or under-class in all societies of religion until you register this reality I am speaking of. You may give up your American citizenship and seek the acceptance of Muslims in Arab lands thinking that you can be your true Muslim self within their reality, but you will find yourself only recognized as the Arabic-speaking foreigner or identified as an Arab-dressing pretender. You may think you have convinced the native people that you belong among them, but they will see you in your true self. I am not speaking of your skin color or your language accent or hair texture. There are Arabs speaking their Arabic dialects... *Shamiy, Masriy, Hejaziy,* whatever they are, with skin blacker and hair kinkier than yours. So, it is not ethnicity or race or skin color or some Wakanda-land fantasy that makes you a special people.

Prophet Muhammed indicated that he was aware of a time when the black people were the ruling authority in the world. He didn't only identify rulership with whites or Arabs. He said plainly, "there is no superiority of a white over a black, or a black over a white, or Arabs over non-Arabs, or non-Arabs over Arabs. The only true distinction is human performance before G'd." So, as a component of nature, if you are an artificial human life imitating human life you will be recognized in your internal conflict, in your denial of your true self. You will be such an imitation that you will search to identify with others even in their shortcomings and weaknesses.

And, if they improve or correct themselves you will insist that they made no error.

Though you will not acknowledge it, you are in an active and self-destructive denial of the fact that G'd did not form you in the same way he formed others. Your physical constitution is the same human form, but you are brought out of that physical form as a select people. G'd says that he forms your physical reality in the stages of physical development, but then He brings you out as another creation.

You have been formed to be a new human creation with a specific human purpose. And there have been no people on this earth like us. It is only when you accept that reality that you become comfortable. When you accept that you have been selected by G'd, and all of what has formed your condition and circumstances are as a result of what G'd intended.

There is no moral or rational answer to explain the degree of rejection and forced subjugation in the spiritual nature of us as a people, where the whole people were destroyed as a human community, destroyed in your natural urges to perform for yourself, except that G'd was recreating you as a new human being. If you refuse to see this, or you actively resist the responsibility to shoulder it and progress within its disciplines, then you will find yourself cursed and under a punishment from G'd.

Allah says that He created for you death, and that it is common property to all that have life. And then he brings you out of death into a reality of which your knowledge runs into its limitations, and you have no reference to measure the possibilities for what has been created anew. This is where the knowledge and language of Imam W. Deen Mohammed defines the life and direction of a new human community.

It should not be expected that a new human creation with Islamic identity would express themselves using language that has been corrupted by at least 450 years of misuse in the Muslim world, and with the present-day Muslim world leadership failing to straighten-out the effects of its own ignorance, sinful excesses, and neglect. The language of this new people will be pure, fresh, and of a clarity so pristine until any mis-statement or misrepresentation clashes so obviously with its truth, that even a person uninitiated in its reasoning will be able to determine the error.

This is why what I am saying is so different from others in its language, reason and emphasis. It is because I was taught by the man himself to reason in his language, to think in his language, and to communicate in his language with the degree of fluency and skilled use that, even while I sit in prison, its validity has proven itself in an obvious and unequivocal way. Accept it or deny it, he authorized, enabled, and trusted my public use of his knowledge in a way unlike any other of his students. The reason is that he wanted it established that there would be no leaders in the community of his people without the sincere and skilled use of his knowledge. To deny his way is to be marked by your own tongue. It is sad and hurtful, but you will find them struggling and weak in their ability to address the needs of his people, utterly incoherent and confused in his knowledge, even though they claim to be advanced students or even masters of the Arabic language and Islamic teaching.

It is because their knowledge is alleged, borrowed, and unsatisfactory for use. They allege it to be true Islamic understanding, but it is actually borrowed from the stores of another peoples' knowledge. Those bases of knowledge address circumstances that don't fit the people of Imam W. Deen Mohammed's purpose, nor do they satisfy the necessary applications of Islamic knowledge for this critical time in mankind's universal reality. They have traded away the superior value of what G'd has given them for universal use in all seasons and for all people, for that which doesn't even permit them an honorable entry or exit. It is in identifying our purpose as a new human community, and addressing our needs in the context of how that signals a new appreciation for the possibilities of a new human world and reality, that we can readily appreciate the value of Imam Mohammed's knowledge.

He would not want that his name be mentioned in any context other than serving the best life of humanity as G'd intended within the context of his people's story and journey.

Not only the African-American people at large, but the specific group, the following, that began with his father's efforts to restore respect and dignity to those people. It is ludicrous to think that the understanding that formed from this people, and this language that speaks and shares that understanding with the world so as to serve the best human interests and highest perceptions and pursuits of human existence and excellence, would not be cherished, preserved, and defended by his people. And so, by living in its substance and exercising its science of application for the human life we earn purity and charitable credits from the Lord-Creator.

What we have is Islamic knowledge and reasoning, but it is that which comes with a new human life. It is the true origin of Islamic knowledge and true conclusions of Islamic reasoning with emphasis to serve a people in their new life. It is the speech of a selected people, who in the full light of human history are known to have been denied their human life identity. What people would be more deserving to carry the Message of Guidance in the modern world than these people?

If we understand the final message to humanity from G'd to be the Holy Qur'an, then it must be a people speaking the Holy Qur'an language in all of its considerations, confirmations, corrections, and completions, but with an appeal to more than ritual understanding and existence. It must be also be an innocent people untutored in the power schemes of worldly authorities. It must be a people without any supportive heritage that could claim and save them. It must be an uncultivated people. It must be an un-named people. It must be an un-valued people. It must be an 'X' people. A people no nation wanted or could lay claim to. A people selected and marked for G'd's purposes.

Perhaps some people reading or hearing this will not have patience with the spiritual nature of what I am referring to. They prefer and are more comfortable with the language of the commercial world, or the political world, or the scientific world. As I said this is spiritual language, but with far-reaching implications. A people awakened to this reality will begin the processes of re-evaluating their existence in every single way they interact with their environment. Every point of entry into society will be affected by their new knowledge and language. They will begin the process of questioning the political language and appeal around them and interpret that language in the context of a new appreciation for their worth as a human being.

They will question the quality of their material existence and place new demands on their income and investigate new possibilities for sources of income. They won't be satisfied with a neighborhood or community existence that falls below their new-found human worth. All because they have recognized for the first time that their condition has been permitted by their Creator, so that they would be enabled to come into a new mind, a new energy, a new human morality all framed within a picture of a new human identity. Perhaps, for the first time, they will understand what a human being is and what the human life has been created for, and they will see how humanity has been separated from this picture, and how they as a member in a selected group have been designated to restore this picture as G'd intended.

This is the life and direction of a people being created as a new human community. This is the language of the people of Imam W. Deen Mohammed. We claim it for ourselves. We claim it in the context of our mission as a people. We claim it for our service to the human life and human identity. We claim it as salvation for the African-American soul.

Special Note from the Author

The author gave the following answer to a question about the use of the phrase 'People of W. Deen Mohammed':

It is not intended to answer those who are enemies of Imam W. Deen Mohammed and his following. Neither is it for those who offer critiques without knowledge or faith. These types of people have negative intentions from the onset, and no matter what clear discussion is presented to them from any source, it does not satisfy their appetite for increasing confusion and forcing unjust burdens upon the Believers. They are full of hate, and they want destruction of the good. They are hypocrites and supporters of wrongdoing and followers of its chief. Allah says that Shaytan commands to evil and shameful acts, and to say of Allah of things of which there is no supporting knowledge.

We intend this statement to serve the best of the People, those who have clean hearts and pure intentions. They deserve our attention and respect, and are entitled to a clear explanation.

It is not advisable or healthy to promote divisions in the human family, and it is especially a sensitive, serious matter to promote or attempt to justify any divisions in the international following of Muhammed the Prophet. However, a recognizable distinction must be drawn between truth and falsehood. The religion of Al-Islam does not accept or legitimize any artificial divisions. As a conscious body of Muslims, we define ourselves as Believers above any other designation. That is to say we are the People of Faith, and we are the People of the Holy Qur'an, and we are the People of Muhammed, we pray to Allah that He bestow upon Muhammed the choicest favor and the peace. These are all descriptions from the Holy Qur'an and the Prophet's teaching.

Allah says that He created us from a common human heritage and that He made us to enjoy the benefits of family lineage and to celebrate that lineage with a humane pride and dignity respecting all others in their lineage, and valuing obedience and regardfulness of Him as the most important component of that human lineage or identity. That which distinguishes man from man, according to Islamic teaching in the Holy Qur'an and Muhammed the Prophet's verified reports, are those qualities and characteristics which qualify as the proper Regardfulness of G'd, and its associated proper and disciplined human thinking and behavior. Informed Muslims know this to be worship. Therefore, it is only correct or incorrect worship that truly distinguishes people from one another in the estimation of G'd.

When we say we are the People of Imam W. Deen Mohammed, we are saying implicitly and simultaneously that we are the People of Faith, the People of the Holy Qur'an, and the People of the Tradition of Muhammed the Prophet. How is this language expressing that? Imam W. Deen Mohammed emphasized that he and his following are a new people on this earth. Honest people looking at us, assessing us, and assessing our use of the Holy Qur'an understanding and language can see this clearly. Learned people in Al-Islam, the ulema, clearly see this. They may not like it, but they see it even more clearly than many of us who embrace it. We have been brought to correct Faith and Practice, not through the teaching of the ulema (many of whom openly and rightly refer to themselves as Salafiyy or followers of the way of the predecessors) of the Arabian peninsula or Indian subcontinent or North Africa, or some other area where there is a density of learned Muslims; but by processes and enlightenment that came unique to our situation in our reality in America.

It is a guided tradition that cannot be separated from the name or person of Imam W. Deen Mohammed and his teaching over 33 public years. We are not ignorant followers. We are conscious, and to say 'People of Imam W. Deen Mohammed' underscores and emphasizes that consciousness. Perhaps 10 years from now this language will not be as necessary because we will have succeeded in our purposes for promoting the public use of Imam W. Deen Mohammed's understanding and are not intimidated or delayed from doing so. It is known that most of the criticism is not because of the use of this phrase, but because the people using it are growing in numbers and because they have identified Imam Earl Abdulmalik Mohammed to lead them in this issue. Just as the ulema insists that Muslims refer to themselves in a way that distinguishes them from the disbelief and oppressive acts of ignorant Muslims in this period of difficulty and trial for Islam in the world, we have made an intelligent choice of language that makes clear who we are and what we are committed to within the following of Muhammed the Prophet.

I can excuse the ignorant, but so-called educated Muslims should be ashamed to criticize our use of 'People of Imam W. Deen Mohammed' when they comfortably use terms as Sunni and Shia, and Hanbaliy and Hanifiy and Shafiy and Malikiy and Wahhabiy and Saudiy, and on and on, when describing or referring to a Muslim nation or community's use of Islamic knowledge in their distinct religious, social, cultural, spiritual, legal, and political realities. No one questions that use. The label 'Muslim' should be sufficient, but we understand the use of these various terms in their real-world context, and they are not disturbing our Islamic unity or dignity. For those understanding the proper use of the

Holy Qur'an's Arabic grammar rules, the term 'Warithuddiniy' would be comprehended very well in the context in which we are saying 'People of Imam W. Deen Mohammed.'

There are many in Imam W. Deen Mohammed's following that choose not to use this description because they are comfortable in their own places and perspectives, or because it is new to them, or because the reasons for its use are unclear. These are honest people. They do not speak on what they do not know or understand. They do not repeat lies or unverified statements, or say irresponsible, vulgar things in public spaces about persons or events they have no knowledge of. I sincerely love them in the way Believers love each other. They do not have to accept me, but I ask them to recognize in Imam Mohammed's words the role and responsibility he intended for me that I have matured to understand and carry out. I want them to know that I understand their point of view and respect it. I support their excellent works and service. I pray to Allah for their success and preservation. I thank Allah for them. They are beautiful in their Islamic life and choices. They are my brothers and sisters in Faith and in family, but my job is different from theirs.

What is necessary for those who identify with the language 'People of Imam W. Deen Mohammed' is distinct from others in terms of role and duty, though we share a common heritage and identity with all Muslims and we share something special with those who identify with Imam W. Deen Mohammed. Allah says that there are ranks and degrees of responsibility and understanding in the applications for progress of Islamic life. There are elevations in perspective and duty. Even the Prophets and Messengers had these ranks and degrees of elevation. Not all of the Prophets and Messengers were given the same uses of knowledge, or the same weight of obligations. Those understanding and using the language 'People of Imam W. Deen Mohammed' have an important degree and elevation of duty to the whole of our group and to Allah, the Most High, and we are committed to use this designation until we are satisfied that it has become unnecessary to continue.

I declare now that the People of Imam W. Deen Mohammed are distinguished from those who knew Imam W. Deen Mohammed's leadership but rejected it by their refusal of his direct and open instructions, and are now cursed and under a punishment for cheating and misrepresenting what he taught and lived for.

"...We brought out from each Ummah (People) a witness, and We brought you out as a witness to these People"

Holy Qur'an 4:41

Statement on March 15, 2019 New Zealand Attacks

Muslim-American Ministry for Human Salvation
Office of the Representative of Imam W. Deen Mohammed,
Imam Earl Abdulmalik Mohammed

STATEMENT ON ATTACKS AGAINST WORSHIPERS IN NEW ZEALAND

Our deepest felt condolences and concerns are extended to the families of those whose lives were lost, and who have been injured, at the hands of terrorists and their assaults on the worshipers at two Mosques in Christchurch, New Zealand during the Friday prayers. We intend this statement also to speak our sincerest sympathies to families affected by similar instances of terrorist assault on all peoples of faith in all nations perpetrated by extremism's corrupted hearts, ugly minds, and sinful hands. An assault on innocence is not ever anticipated. Even in this present world of human communities having serious difficulties understanding each other, the human heart is not inclined and does not naturally prepare itself for an attack on worship. We seek the Help of Allah with this and all matters that confound us, that our human world struggles with and must define, defend against, and ultimately prevent. As Muslims, we know that Islam is human community in peaceful worship of the Lord-Creator, and that this and all similar attacks against worshipers target human community innocence. In obeying our disciplines of faith we turn to Guidance and common sense to characterize what we see, experience, and endure in our world. We do not conclude any causes for such horror before we ask Allah for relief, and then we pursue the better judgments, lessons, and understanding with His Mercy. Our thoughts are for all of the people of New Zealand, and prayers that they will show all of us the blessed human demonstration of love and care for neighbors and countrymen in need.

Index

A

Abbas, Ibn, 19-20

Abdel-Nasser, Gamel, 90

Abraham, 16-17, 37, 93

Adam, 16-17, 19, 31, 37-38, 79, 94, 97-98, 104-105, 124

Africa, xv, 5, 9, 29-30, 48, 69-70, 90-91, 125, 137

African-Americans, 24, 37-38, 46, 52, 126

Afrikaner, 91

Al-Aqsa, Masjid, xxvi

al-Khattab, Umar bin, 114

Ali Jinnah, Muhammad, 90

Ali, Muhammad 78

Arabic language, xv, 49, 125, 131

Arabs, 36, 124-125, 129

As-Siddiq, Abu Bakr, 20

Asia, xv, 90

B

Bangladesh, 72

Bilalian, iii, viii, xix-xx, xxv, 38, 73

Black Church, 15

Black Lives Matter, 86

black nationalism, 97

black stone, 127

Burma, xxvi, 94, 124

C

Central America, 52

chattel slavery, 38

China, 94, 124

Christians, xxviii, 30-31, 47-48, 89, 117

citizenship, xiii, xxvii, 23, 35, 37-38, 44, 47-48, 60, 72-73, 87, 94, 97-99, 128

Civil War, 53

colonization, 57, 90

Crusades, 89-91

Cuba, 125

D

David, 61

Day of Religion, i, iii, vii-viii, xi-xii, xvi, xx, 30, 56, 81

E

Egypt, 72, 90-91

Ellis Island, 48

Enemy of man, 3, 21, 48, 78-79

entitlements, xxiii, 27, 32, 35-37, 89,

97, 122

equality, 14, 57, 73, 95, 128

F

Fard, W. D., 46, 96, 122

Farrakhan, Louis, 22

Focolare, 24

Forbes Forum, 72

Founders, 14, 33-34, 39, 45, 53, 98

Franco, Francisco, 90

freedom, i, 1, 4-6, 8, 45, 57, 73-74, 95, 111, 114-115, 118

G

Gaza, 60

Germany, 48, 60, 90, 125

Gulen, Fethullah, 24

H

Haram, Shareef, xxvi

Harlem, 22-23

holocaust, 48, 60

human community, xi, xx, 7, 10, 19, 51-52, 94, 112, 116, 121, 123-124, 127, 130-131, 133

I

immigrant, 24, 67, 70, 119

imperialism, 90

India, 72

intellect, xxi, 5-7, 16-17, 32, 34, 101, 106, 118, 124

interfaith, xx, 103, 106

Iraq, 91, 94

Islamic State, 94

Israel, xxv-xxviii

J

Jerusalem, xxv-xxvii, 37, 93

Jesus Christ, 96

Jews, 31, 47-48, 89-90, 117

jihad, xvi, 36, 94-96

Jim-Crow, 14

Joseph, 118

just establishments, 1, 114, 116-117

justice, xi-xii, xxvi, 29, 45, 56-57, 61, 73, 95

K

Ka'aba, xxvii

khalifa, 19

L

Libya, 72

Lubich, Chiara, 24

M

Madinah, xxvii

Makkah, xxvii, 5, 12, 37

Malcolm X, 22

Mary, Maryam, 30, 31, 91, 101, 112

materialism, 37

Mexico, 47

Middle East, xv, 90

militarism, 95

Moses, 93, 114, 117

Muhammad, Elijah, xxi, 65, 69, 84, 92, 97, 119, 122

Muhammad's Temple of Islam, 49, 120, 123

Muhammed the Prophet, v, xi, xix, xxiii, xxv, 2-3, 5, 8, 13, 15, 18, 33, 35-36, 47, 57-59, 65, 78, 85, 92, 101, 112, 114-115, 123-124, 127,

135-137

Mohammed, W. Deen (Wallace D. Mohammed, Warithuddin Mohammed), i, ix, xv-xvi, xviii-xxi, xxv, 2-3, 9, 12, 17, 20-26, 30, 32-33, 36, 44, 46-47, 52-53, 56, 58, 64-66, 69-70, 72-73, 76, 79, 84-86, 92, 96-99, 107, 109-110, 112, 115, 117, 121, 123-124, 130-131, 133, 135-139

Muhammad, W. F., 4

Muslim-American, i, iii, vii-viii, xv-xvi, xviii-xxi, 15, 22-24, 47, 68, 71-73, 78, 92, 99, 128

Muslim-Americans, i, xv, 23, 51, 66-67, 70, 73, 84, 98-99

Myanmar, 124

N

Nation of Islam, 2, 22, 52, 96-97, 122

nationalism, i, xx, xxiii, 8, 83, 86, 88, 90-91, 93-97, 117

Native Americans, 44, 124, 128

Nazi, 48, 60

New America, 39

New World Patriotism Day, 73

New York Times, 22

New Zealand, 141

North Africa, 90, 137

O

oppression, xii, 3, 6, 8, 10, 46, 61, 75, 88-90, 123-124, 126

P

Pakistan, 90

Palestinians, 59

patriotism, i, xx, 33, 35-36, 39, 47, 52-

53, 73, 96, 98-99

peace, i, xvii, xxvii, 1, 3, 12, 17, 27-28, 30, 37, 43-44, 47, 55-57, 59, 61, 63-64, 66, 83-84, 89, 92, 101-102, 114, 116, 119-121, 123, 136

People of the Book, 47

R

racism, 68, 117

Ramadan, 56, 108

ritual, 27, 61-62, 65, 107, 132

Robert Mugabe, 91

Rohingya, xxvi, 59, 124

Rome, 90

S

Saddam Hussein, 91

Salafiyy, 136

Saudi Arabia, xv, xxvii

self-determination, xxviii, 95

Shabazz, Malcolm, 22

Shariah, 95

slavery, 9, 32, 38, 45, 69, 87, 116, 120, 123, 126

social destiny, 88

socialism, 90

South Africa, 91

Spain, 90

Sudan, 72

Supreme Court, 34

Syria, 91, 94

systems of knowledge, xii, xvii, xix, 8, 13, 101, 110, 117

T

The Heritage Foundation, 72

Turkey, 24

U

ulema, 21, 136-137

United Arab Republic, 90

United States Constitution, 4, 45, 67, 98

universal justice, xi, 29

universal rights, xxvi-xxvii

Uyghurs, 124

V

Voice of America, 72

W

Wakanda, 129

Wahhabiy, 137

Washington, D.C., 49

World Community of al-Islam in the West, 96

Y

Yemen, xv, 94

9 781733 603409